FROM THE WESTERN FRONT TO SALONIKA

A FRENCH SOLDIER WRITES HOME

Letters of Pierre Suberviolle (1914-1919)

Edited by Catherine Labaume-Howard

Translation by Hugh Nicklin

Helion & Company

This book is dedicated
· to my mother
· to Linda Hart

"... a letter is like a kiss or caress which gives my soul back a little of the affection which it misses so much. It gives me courage and good spirits. Exchanging letters makes it possible for our souls to speak to each other, and I can imagine that I'm there with you again."
—Pierre Suberviolle (Salonika, April 15th 1917)

"Here is the reason why I like so much dairies, personal writings, letters... When you read these texts, you feel that an unknown person is there, at your side, that he has a liking for you and chosen you as a confidant. And it is fascinating to hear what he has to tell you, to penetrate into his intimacy, to live again and relish what he has experienced and that his words glorify".
—Charles Juliet, *Lumières d'automne* (1946)

Quelle connerie la guerre ("What shit war is")
—Jacques Prévert, 'Barbara', *Paroles* (1946)

Helion & Company Limited
26 Willow Road
Solihull
West Midlands
B91 1UE
England
Telephone 0121 705 3393
Fax 0121 711 4075
Email: publishing@helion.co.uk
Website: www.helion.co.uk
Twitter: @helionbooks
Visit our blog http://blog.helion.co.uk/

Published by Helion & Company 2016
First published in 2011, under the title *Lettres de la "der des der" – Les lettres à Mérotte: correspondance de Pierre Suberviolle (1914-1918)*, by La Louve Editions, BP 225 – 46004 Cahors, ISBN 978-2-916488-43-1

Designed and typeset by Farr out Publications, Wokingham, Berkshire
Cover designed by Paul Hewitt, Battlefield Design (www.battlefield-design.co.uk)
Printed by Hobbs The Printers Ltd, Totton, Hampshire

Front cover image: Augusta and Paulette Suberviolle. (Private collection)
Rear cover image: The author and the editor of the letters, October 1941. (Private collection)

ISBN 978-1911096-28-3

British Library Cataloguing-in-Publication Data.

A catalogue record for this book is available from the British Library.

For details of other military history titles published by Helion & Company Limited contact the above address, or visit our website: http://www.helion.co.uk.

We always welcome receiving book proposals from prospective authors.

Contents

List of images

Preface

It gives me great pleasure to introduce this selection of letters written by French soldier Pierre Suberviolle. Madame Labaume-Howard has diligently compiled an interesting selection of her grandfather's letters, which should attract our attention for several reasons.

First, there are not many first-hand accounts by either members of the French transport service (*Direction de Service Automobile* – DSA) or the French tank service (the *Artillerie Spéciale* – *AS*). In addition, the campaign in Salonika has received little general or scholarly attention and, indeed, had little attention paid to it during the war (see p. 88, for example). By coincidence, one of the other *AS* veterans who has left us his memoirs, Maurice Constantin-Weyer, also joined the *AS* after service in Salonika.

In addition, Pierre's letters help dispel the idea that the war was an unrelenting hell for those on the Western Front. During this terrible war, young men continued to be interested in young women, as Pierre's developing relationship with Marie-Antoinette Barthe charmingly illustrates, and they continued to have the other interests that young men throughout history have had, in Pierre's case mainly wine, money and tobacco. As Pierre wrote on attending officer school: 'It is the end of my career as a party animal!' (p. 110-11).

Pierre joined the *AS* at an interesting time in early 1918, as the organisation was shifting its emphasis from the unwieldy medium tanks to the revolutionary light Renault tanks. Madame Labaume-Howard mentions in her introduction that Pierre often felt he should be more active on the frontline itself (p. xix), which raises an issue that many modern readers will be unfamiliar with: the scarcity of drivers during the war. While being able to drive is a fairly prosaic skill in the modern world, this was not the case during the Great War. Prior to the war, few people knew how to drive motor vehicles and this skill became increasingly important as motor transport in the French army increased substantially during the war, largely as a result of the large numbers of horses killed in 1914 and 1915.

This problem was compounded when the French began their tank programme in 1916 and would remain an issue for the remainder of the war. (This is why Pierre's mother had such trouble getting a competent driver during the war, mentioned in a letter she wrote to Pierre, quoted on page xvii). Competent drivers were thus at a premium and it is not surprising that the French army used Pierre's skills to both drive and then instruct other soldiers in this art, rather than deploy him as an infantryman or artilleryman. By the time that Pierre joined the *AS*, he had accrued great experience as a driver, as well as uncommon knowledge of vehicle repair while with the French Eastern Army (see pp. 103 and 112). Despite his clear skill in teaching, Pierre got his wish and eventually got into combat with the 12th battalion of light tanks, where he demonstrated great valour.

I will not ruin the reader's journey by unveiling the denouement of Pierre's military career but suffice it to say that he meets adversity with his customary good humour and stoicism. These carefully chosen letters wonderfully illustrate the human capacity to endure suffering and hardship without losing our basic humanity and I recommend them to anyone interested in the First World War.

Tim Gale, London, August 2016
Author of *The French Army Tank Force and Armoured Warfare in the Great War* (2013)

Foreword

It all started with a cache of letters in a potato sack, stuffed in the back of a cupboard and only brought to light when the family moved house. They proved to be a soldier's letters home from the First World War. The writer of the letters, Pierre Suberviolle, was born in September 1896, and thus became 18 just after the outbreak of the war. During the 51 months that the war lasted he maintained correspondence with several family members – his mother Augusta, his sister Paulette, his father Louis and his grandparents. The outbreak of war had interrupted his college course at the Toulouse University Science Faculty, where he had been studying Veterinary Science. This was in expectation that he would follow his father and grandfather into the family veterinary practice, a flourishing enterprise in a world of town and country in which horses were still widely used for transport.

Pierre joined up (without his father's knowledge) on 7 August 1914. It was just three days after the war broke out, and he was at that date still only 17. He was assigned to the transport corps as a driver/mechanic, and served for a year and a half supplying the troops on the Western Front. He was then transferred to the 'French Eastern Army' at Salonika, criss-crossing Albania, Macedonia and Greece in the course of its Balkan campaign. Transferred back to France in October 1917, he became a tank driver, and was hit in the face in combat near Dunkirk just three weeks before the armistice. As a result of this injury he lost an eye, but this did not prevent him marrying his childhood sweetheart Marie-Antoinette Barthe.

Like most young French soldiers, Pierre wrote to his mother all through the war. She represented his roots and a fixed point in his life. She was the woman in whose image, (and sometimes in contrast to it), he formed his own personality. So close were his links to 'Mémère' or 'Mérotte' (his pet names for her) that he was aware of the danger that he might never have the time to form a lasting relationship with any other woman. She remained until further notice, and for the duration of the war, the woman in his life. The closeness of their relationship was intensified after the death of his father in 1916 as a result of being kicked in the head by a skittish horse.

Pierre Suberviolle continued to 'chat', as he put it, with his mother all through the war. He confided to her his moments of joy and disaster; he told her of his state of mind, his love for rural beauty, his bouts of depression and his money worries. Dimly, reading between the lines, we make out the outlines of fleeting adventures with girls and women who 'get their claws into him'. We can understand and forgive the amorous adventures of a young man who acknowledges that he has 'had a devil in him' and has yielded more to the demands of his hormones than to those of his heart.

Pierre's main preoccupation is to put his mother's mind at rest (the letters of the writer Jean Giono tell a similar story); he makes an effort to hide from her the real horrors of the Front, which he described more fully in his letters to Mr Barthe, his future father-in-law. Marie-Antoinette destroyed some of these letters in 1986, shocked by the violence they described.

After the death of his father Pierre became the head of the family. His attitude to his sister passed through phases, first a young man's appreciation of her developing feminine charms, and later an older brother's solicitous regard for a young sister needing a protective father figure in the absence of her real father now deceased.

From 1917 Pierre kept up a secret correspondence with Marie-Antoinette Barthe, the girl he would marry after the war. This was rudely interrupted at her father's insistence, who would not entertain a marriage project while the war continued to make the future so unpredictable.

In publishing her maternal grandfather's letters, 48 years after his death, Catherine Labaume-Howard has struck a wonderful blow for the value of correspondence. Whether on paper or on the computer screen, a letter remains "a kiss" or a "caress", an essential element in the "communion of souls" which Pierre evokes in his letter of 15 April 1917. Our present day egotistic society is in dire need of such "communion of souls", and it is important for the future of humanity that we promote it as much as we can.

Jean-Pierre Guéno[1]

This Foreword appeared in the French edition of the book, published by La Louve Editions in 2011 under the title *Lettres de la 'der des der' – Les lettres à Mérotte: correspondance de Pierre Suberviolle (1914-1918)*.

---

1   Jean-Pierre Guéno is a French author/historian. His celebrated *Paroles de Poilus* (1998) – a collection of French soldiers' 1914-18 letters – is utilised in schools throughout France. (Note: Henceforth translator's notes will be denoted [T's N]).

Acknowledgements

This book is dedicated to my mother, Jacqueline Suberviolle-Labaume, who saved and classified all of her father's letters after they were discovered. Her personal memories were a great help in supplementing the letters and helping to explain some of them. Many special thanks to:

- Duncan Rogers and Dr Michael LoCicero at Helion for their support and helpful suggestions.
- My French publisher La Louve Editions and Jean-Louis Marteil, for his valuable help and enthusiasm.
- Jean-Pierre Guéno, writer and journalist, a First World War specialist (author of the famous *Paroles de Poilus)* who believed in my project, gave me the energy to complete it and wrote the preface to the French edition.
- Dr Tim Gale, a noted authority on First World War French armoured forces, for providing additional information and composing an illuminating Preface.
- Linda Hart, for her meticulous proofreading, and for providing the crucial link between myself in the south of France and Helion in the English Midlands.
- My translator Hugh Nicklin, who not only did a beautiful translation but also added useful footnotes.
- Dominique Labaume, whose help was essential in exploring family archives and photo albums.
- Stéphane Dugué and Gilbert Polonovski who did a great job retouching old photos.
- Jacques Regaud who sent me the Barthes' archives.
- Catherine McLean who was the very first one to point out what a treasure the letters were and that they deserved to become a book.
- Danielle Deloche for her friendship and valuable help.

And last but not least, thanks to my husband whose attentive ear, patience and help on the computer made this book possible.

Catherine Labaume-Howard
Castelnaudary, France 2016

Introduction

Pierre Suberviolle (1897–1964) was my grandfather on my mother's side. I knew him very well, since I was 24 when he died. I not only knew him, but loved him dearly, because he was the first "man in my life". I was born in his house – on 34 Emile Pouvillon Street, in Montauban[1], the address to which he sent almost all his letters.

My parents had married in August 1939, just before the war broke out; my father, a young officer who had just graduated from the military school at Saint-Cyr had to go back to his battalion three days after the wedding, and my mother went back to her parents' house. I was conceived during a leave, but my mother spent the whole war on Pouvillon street, so Pierre was like a father to me.

The situation recurred from 1949 to 1952, when my father had to go to fight in Indochina. With my mother, my three brothers and sisters and I came back to live in the big family house at Montauban. I have many vivid memories of that time, particularly of the day in 1951 when Mamé (Pierre's mother) died at the age of 75. I was playing in the garden and my ball rolled into Pierre's office: when he heard me, he came out, embraced me and began to cry, saying "I'm very sad, because my Mum has died and I loved her so much." I was eleven, and dumbfounded to see my granddad crying like a kid, but when I read the letters he sent her from 1914 to 1918, I understood.

Where do these letters come from?

The Suberviolle family had a little country house in Saint-Clar, near Muret.[2] It was sold in 1986 after the death of Pierre's younger sister, Paulette, who had inherited it. When the house was cleared, somebody found a potato sack in a cupboard. In it was a large bundle of letters still in their envelopes. They were all the letters Pierre had sent during the First World War, not only to his mother, but to his sister, his father and his grand-parents. As well as the letters there were postcards, death announcements, letters from friends – anything which bore on the topics mentioned in the correspondence. It was almost certainly Pierre's mother herself who kept all the letters together. The whole collection – more than 300 letters – was given to my mother, who read them, and she mentioned them to me. At that time in my life I had no time to spend studying them, nor did the task much appeal to me. It was only when I retired and had more leisure that I took a friend's advice and opened the sack again. Then the adventure began.

To whom was Pierre writing?

As one would expect, most of the letters are to his Suberviolle relatives. A few are to Antonin Barthe, a friend of the family whose daughter Pierre married. Any letters he wrote to friends were not, of course, available to be collected by his mother.

---

1   Thirty-five miles north of Toulouse [T's N]
2   South of Toulouse [T's N]

Pierre aged approximately 12 or 13. (Private collection)

Les Suberviolles

Pierre was the son of Louis Suberviolle (1871-1916), a vet, and his wife Augusta Viguier (1876-1951). He had a young sister, Paulette (1902-1985). They lived in a large house with a garden in Montauban, with Augusta's parents, François Viguier, who was also a vet, and his wife Albanie. Pierre had a comfortable and happy childhood, in a typical 19th century provincial bourgeois milieu, with peasant roots not far away. These were the days before motorcars, and vets prospered looking after people's horses.

Pierre went to school in Montauban until he was 15, but for his "baccalauréat"[3](1911-1912), his parents sent him instead to the Lycée Pierre-de-Fermat[4] in Toulouse. During his time there Pierre stayed at the nearby student accommodation hostel of Sainte-Barbe, managed by the Assumptionist Fathers, an order of Catholic priests. Pierre's mother's collection of letters includes some written by Pierre at this time. He assured her that he was working hard, but he still failed his exams. Pierre's parents then sent him to board at a Lycée in Cahors. He studied Biological Sciences, evidently planning to follow the family tradition by becoming a vet.

He worked harder, and in October 1913 gained the diploma enabling him to register as a student at the Science University in Toulouse for the academic year 1913–14. He was seventeen years old. Hardly any of the letters in the collection refer to this year in Toulouse, which was close enough to Montauban for him to go home frequently. In 1913 he passed

---

3   French exam roughly equivalent to A level [T's N]
4   Named after the famous 17th century mathematician Fermat, a former pupil of the University of Toulouse. It has been described as the "oldest and most prestigious high school" in Toulouse [T's N]

The Suberviolles – (standing) Pierre, Augusta, Paulette in nurse's uniform, Louis (seated) François and Albanie Viguier, Augusta's parents (1916). (Private collection)

his driving test, having had lessons with his father in their brand new 10 HP Renault.

The letters from the teenage Pierre reveal many of his traits as an adult: he is loving and anxious to please his parents; he likes good food and is fastidious about his appearance and personal hygiene (three letters contain requests for Cologne, for example!). He has an open disposition and a good sense of humour.

It is not easy to understand Pierre's father, the vet Louis Suberviolle. The letters Louis sent to his wife from Brest in Brittany (where he was sent on military duty in 1914) are not much help. He describes his military duties: he works with horses (still numerous in the army) and supervises slaughterhouses and meat canneries. He speaks of his touching love for his wife, and provides details of train bookings he has organized for her to visit him. He gives (in response to his wife's request) details of his expenses. He speaks of his dog and horse-riding. He also talks of his diet, which he has been trying to follow for some time. This comes out in one of Pierre's letters from Cahors:

6 January 1913
Yesterday morning the Headmaster died suddenly. It made a big impression on me, because he was only 47 and had visited the dormitories only the night before. As you know, he ate and drank a lot and smoked like a chimney, so his death didn't come as a complete surprise to us. I mention it for Dad's sake, to encourage him to behave himself, stick rigidly to his diet and follow every detail of what the doctor prescribes. Then we can stop worrying about him.

Louis Suberviolle c.1910. (Private collection)

Was Louis overdoing the 'good life'? In some letters he mentions that he draws pictures to while away the time. After his death his collection of drawings was found; they were neat pen-and-ink drawings, inspired by photos in magazines and newspapers[5]. In Montauban his hobby had been cabinet-making: some of his reproduction antique furniture is still in the family home. For a middle-class man, he had quite an artistic streak.

And what can one say about his wife Augusta, 'Little Mum' as Pierre calls her? She was evidently a woman of strong character, sometimes even a bit of a tyrant. She adored her son with an exclusive and jealous love. She worried a lot about her husband's health. Here she is, writing to their friend Antonin Barthe after Louis had been home on leave:

19 August 1915
Since he has gone back to his old ways of eating, drinking and smoking, he's in bad shape ... Although he's only just gone back, I'm going to take Paulette with me to be with him again. It is absolutely vital that I spend time with him to wean him off his bad habits and make him stick to his diet.

This would not be easy, as she was a working woman – with her husband away, she had to keep the vet practice going with her father's help. She looked after everything, as this letter shows:

---

5   One of Louis's drawings. See Chapter 2.

12 January 1915

After the problems with the cleaner we had problems with the car. The chauffeur has been called up: we replaced him with a Belgian who had had a few lessons and thought he was competent to drive and maintain the car. Our confidence was misplaced: he seriously damaged the car by not lubricating it properly, and then missed the fact that there was a leak in the fuel pipe. In the end I had to maintain the car myself to take the worry off Dad's shoulders. I've learned how it works, and after three lessons I'm well on the way to being able to drive it. My uncle is a good driver, and he's coming to see us soon, so I hope he'll perfect my skills.

Augusta managed the money carefully. She was very concerned about her children's education and future careers. After her husband's death in 1916 she became even more solicitous about Pierre's welfare. I include two of her letters from the early and late periods of the war, which bear closely on her personality.

The Barthes

In addition to the letters which Pierre's mother kept, there is also a (much smaller) batch of letters kept by the Barthe family. Sometimes these Barthe letters helped me to understand things which Pierre's letters only hinted at. Antonin and Elisabeth Barthe were close friends of the Suberviolles, and Antonin and Louis were also professional colleagues as vets. They lived at Mas-Grenier, 25 km from Montauban. (When Pierre writes 'Mas' in his letter, it is

Antonin and Elisabeth Barthe c.1910. (Private collection)

Mas-Grenier he is referring to). The Barthes had two daughters, Marie-Antoinette, born in 1897, and Marguerite, born in 1909. The house they lived in is still owned by the family, though the one in Montauban was sold when Augusta died. In 1914 Antonin was called up and sent to Quimper in Brittany. From there he was moved to Bretigny, near Versailles, and his family went up there to join him. They rented the porter's lodge at the Chateau Lafontaine. Pierre himself was seventeen when he went off to war, and Marie-Antoinette was sixteen. They knew each other, but were they also perhaps already fond of each other? Pierre's letters will show us how things developed!

These then are the principal characters in the drama, played out, of course, against the backdrop of the war.

The War

The war makes its presence felt in all the letters. It is the focus of all the evils, fears, emotions and suffering which Pierre experiences during his four years as a soldier, but at the same time it provides him with some happy times. It is very much *his* war which we live through in his letters, although surprisingly few of them refer to incidents of actual combat. Considering that Pierre was primarily a driver, initially of lorries and finally of tanks, it is not surprising that we do not find details of life in the trenches. We do find accounts of periods when he was away from the front, training or waiting for a posting; at those times he was bored and depressed. His family found two of his letters sufficiently striking to have them published in the local newspaper, the Tarn-and-Garonne edition of the *Indépendant*. When I tried to find some context for these incidents, my search was made more difficult because of the censors' requirement that no place-names or other items of potential value as military intelligence be included in soldiers' letters. This is well illustrated by the postcard of the *poilu*[6] writing home: 'We've come from (blank) and are just on our way to (blank) (I can't say where). I'm not ill or wounded and everything is fine ... '

Pierre was attached to the 20th Transport Squadron, which was occupied in carrying food, munitions and trenching materials up to the line, and bringing back the wounded (and unwounded). The squadron was on the road continuously, having to service the needs of several combat formations. Even professional historians often give up on the task of tracing the precise movements of such transport units.

For the time that Pierre served in the Balkans, the marching orders of the French Eastern Army are collected together in a single document which classifies operations month by month chronologically, rather than by unit. Appendix III provides a brief account of the Balkan campaign. I have found the details of his last posting (with the 504th Regiment of Assault Artillery) between August and October 1918. I have also been able to reconstruct the movements of his company (336th); these are recounted in Appendix V.

We should note that Pierre had to endure two long periods of inactivity, one before his Balkan posting during the early months of 1916, and the other after his return from Salonika, during the winter and spring of 1917-18. He had to undergo training in vehicle maintenance and later on in tanks. He says that he was 'ambushed' and was indignant at being taken from the front, but perhaps he was secretly acknowledging that it was partly his decision, as anything else would not accord with his character. Certainly as far as the second period of time is concerned it is possible that, after the death of his father, Pierre began to

---

6   Hairy One: Soldier slang for ordinary French soldier; "Tommy" for the British soldier; "Doughboy" for an
      American soldier. [T's N]

A French *Poilu* writing home. (Private collection)

feel that he owed it to his family to survive for their sake, and so not to take risks. Was his career being manipulated to this end by his family members? The French call the practice of doing career favours 'pistoning' and Pierre's assignment to a transport rather than a front line combat unit could well have been an example of this in practice. Nevertheless he regularly found himself under fire in his lorry at various places between the North Sea and the mountains of Macedonia, and also at the end of the war in his tank. He always showed exemplary courage and insisted that 'I don't want to skulk about behind the lines – it's disgusting'.

The originality of Pierre's letters is that they are not just another view of trench life. Even if the historical content is not very detailed, the reader can still enter into the heart and soul of a man caught up in the tempest, as millions of others, and kept away from home by extremely violent winds. Pierre's perspective is the more valuable because it is unlike most others': therefore his letters are precious, showing us war in an unexpectedly psychological and social way.

So, then, what do the letters relate?

Firstly, family matters: the Suberviolles were a very close family given to regular expressions of their mutual warm affection. My mother remembers this, but also that it was punctuated by quarrels and hard words. Family affection is a constant theme running through the letters, which were the only bright spot in Pierre's life. Whenever an expected letter failed to turn up he was immediately cast down. The reader may weary of the incessant repetition of affectionate formulae, but should recall that there were quite long intervals between letters, and no doubt some never arrived. Pierre also shows his commitment to the family by his concern for the household budget, especially after the death of his father. He gives advice on household matters, the purchase of cars and his little sister's education. We are given a snapshot of the inner life of a French middle class family of that time.

The letters address Pierre's state of mind, and in doing so touch us most deeply. Whenever he can snatch a moment, even if it's in the middle of the night, he settles down to

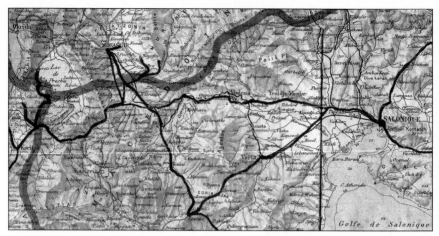

Map of Northern Greece on which Pierre marked all his journeys. (Private collection)

'a bit of a chat', to share his thoughts, puzzles and worries. We hear his views on nature, love, the passing of childhood and the uncertain future, expressed with humour and poetry. We note that when he speaks of matters of the heart he addresses his mother as his 'big sister'.

As to the reality of his everyday life, Pierre often speaks about money. Without being a spendthrift he hated counting pennies. At the beginning he insisted that he needs nothing, but experience soon taught him otherwise. Inflation was continually reducing the purchasing power of his wages. Between 1914 and 1918 the franc fell steadily, and by the end of the war it was worth only half what it had been at the beginning. A yearly subscription to the period picture magazine *L'Illustration*, which had cost 40 francs at the beginning of the war, cost 80 francs at the end of it. If Pierre wanted to eat well, drink anything other than water, smoke his pipe, keep clean, wrap himself up against the foul weather or have a beer with the lads, his soldier's pay needed subsidizing from home. He sent frequent appeals for money, supporting them with little statements of income and expenses which are entertaining to read and revealing. His mother sometimes expresses reservations about the amount, but never refuses.

The business of deciphering and copying Pierre's letters was an adventure in itself. I did not begin by a complete read-through, but dealt with them at the rate of five or six a day, so that I was kept in a long-drawn-out period of suspense, wondering what would happen to my soldier next! It was a roller-coaster emotional ride as his letters were sad, funny and poetic by turns.

They were written on every conceivable medium: we find big sheets of lined paper, pre-stamped army postcards, sheets torn from a note pad, black lined paper (for sad occasions), and postcards he bought in shops. Some are grey, some blue, some off-white and some mauve. I soon got better at reading his handwriting, which is sloping, tightly organised and pressed into the paper when he had time, but a chaotic scribble when he was in a hurry or upset. Some are in black, blue or violet ink, and some in black or violet pencil.

He could express himself well when he took the trouble. Sometimes he wrote as he talked (which he describes as 'chatting'), but at moments of exaltation he adopted a powerfully poetic and evocative style, which is there for all to see in the un-edited letters. His spelling sometimes leaves a lot to be desired and his punctuation is fanciful where not

Military issue postcard. (Private collection)

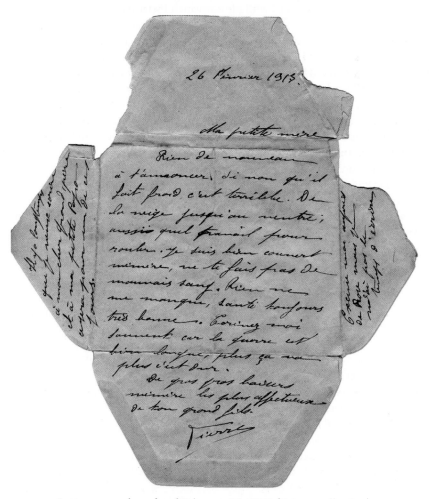

Letter on envelope dated February 26, 1917. (Private collection)

completely absent, and I've taken the liberty of correcting both for him. I have left the punctuation alone as much as possible, especially when he uses exclamation marks and lines of dots to get across the emotion he feels.

I have selected 156 letters out of the total of 300. Many of those I excluded are short, simply letting them know that he is still alive, and many (particularly from the first two years of the war) repeat themselves, so that I could leave them out without losing anything important. In some cases I summarized their contents to keep the narrative thread intact. I've included some details from the letters which, though not directly about Pierre, offer interesting supplementary information. Where I felt it necessary I have added explanatory notes of my own: italicised passages in the letters themselves show where Pierre had underlined things. I hope he would not be offended that I have spared the reader his long farewell formula ("I finish with big hugs for you, Paulette, Granny and Grandpa"), simply adding 'etc'!

Finding pictures for the books was also something of an adventure. I trawled through family photo albums well stocked with photos which Pierre had taken himself; there were also documents and postcards which he included with his letters, and I added some photos, pictures and cards from the time. I also went through a collection of the weekly magazine *Le Miroir* (*The Mirror*) for 1914-17. It always carried a page of news (French triumphs and German defeats!) followed by fifteen pages of pictures, either photos or drawings. Swamped with images of all kinds as we are today, we need to recognise how precious such pictures were to people in those days. They were hard to come by, as the message on the front page of *Le Miroir* confirms: 'We pay any price for interesting war pictures'. *Le Miroir* did a good job, and was a gold-mine for me. Also valuable was *Lectures pour tous* (Readings for All), published between 1914-16, which, though lacking the wealth of *Le Miroir* images, contained a plethora of useful documentary material.

What we find in this correspondence is a view of the war-time experience of a specific social class, a slice of life and the portrait of the young man who was my grandfather. I recognised in the letters all the features of his character which I loved in him: friendly, generous, a party animal, brave, appreciative of feminine charm, dapper and funny – but at the same time capable of plain speaking when angry and sometimes unhappy and even bitter. It is nice to think that those who knew him will recognise him in this book and that other people will find a way into history by the little door represented by a single human destiny.

Catherine Labaume-Howard

੨৯

A note about currency
To help understand Pierre's needs for cash during the war, here is what the French franc would be worth in pounds sterling today.

1 franc in 1914 = £ 2.75 (in 2016)
1 franc in 1918 = £ 1.32 (in 2016)

So when Pierre lists his expenses, in 1918, and they total 100F (see page 164), this would be approximately £132 today.

Chronology

1914
- Pierre Suberviolle volunteers on 7 August at the age of 17½.
- During the autumn and winter he is deployed in eastern France near Saint-Dizier, Villars-Cotterets and Vitry-le-François.

1915
- During the spring and summer Pierre is stationed in the north of France near Dunkirk and Ypres.
- Granted a month's leave for the first time, he returns to Montauban to celebrate his nineteenth birthday in September.
- Returns to active service in northern of France.

1916
- From January to March Pierre is stationed away from the war zone near Versailles, waiting for a posting.
- In March he has a short leave.
- Posted to the French Eastern Army, on 21 March he embarks for Salonika from Toulon.
- Granted compassionate leave in September following the death of his father the previous August.
- Returns to Salonika in early October.

1917
- For most of the year until the end of September Pierre is deployed in Albania, Macedonia and Greece.
- Home leave in October is followed by transfer to Versailles, from where he is posted to Rupt-sur-Moselle in the Vosges sector. He receives engineering training with a view to promotion, finishing at the top of the course and is promoted to corporal.

1918
- On 17 February Pierre is transferred from the Vosges front to Orleans, where he receives tank training at Cercottes Camp. He is sent as an instructor to Gidy Camp, and is promoted to Warrant Officer.
- On 20th July he is sent into action near Dunkirk in command of a pair of tanks.
- Wounded in action on 15 October.
- Treated in the hospital at Zuydcoote, and finally sent to Rouen.
- Returns to Montauban on 13 November.

1

The truck was shaken by a blast

1914
4 August: Germany declares war on France.

19-23 August: Failure of the French Lorraine offensive. Heavy casualties: on 22 August 27,000 French soldiers die in battle.

6-13 September: First battle of the Marne. The famous "Marne taxis"[1] bring troops toward the front. The German armies withdraw. During the autumn, the war of movement settles down to static trench warfare. The front – Arras, Reims, Verdun-Saint-Mihiel, Pont-à-Mousson, Saint-Dié – extends from the English Channel to Switzerland.

20 October–17 November: First Battle of Ypres. The German reverse marks the end of the so-called 'Race to the sea'.

16 December: French attempt a breakthrough in Artois, but are halted on the third day.

1915
15 February–18 March: Failure of a French Champagne offensive.

In August 1914, Louis Suberviolle was called up straight away and sent to the veterinary services at Brest (Brittany). Young Pierre wanted to join up as well, but he would not be 18 until 29 September and needed his father's approval, which was not forthcoming! His grandfather Viguier, a veteran of the 1870–71 war thirsting for revenge, forged Louis' signature so Pierre could enlist.

(On the headed notepaper of Café Georges – Dijon – H.Simonet – Tel 278.)

Dijon, Thursday 13 August 1914
My dear Mum,
We've finally arrived in Dijon, our base, from which we'll go who knows where. It's great to wear the uniform, but it's not very comfortable.

Up to now, I could only eat a bit of cheese, some "monkey"[2] and bread. I'm not complaining, though, and am enjoying my new life. Everybody treats me as a kid, and I can purloin sausage, coffee and sugar, so that I am never unhappy.

We saw our first anti-aircraft guns set up in a battery and ready to shoot, as air attacks are expected. I hope to hear the shooting soon.

---

1   General Galliéni famously requisitioned all of the Paris taxis to transport troops to the front.[T's N]
2   Military jargon for meat (T's N)

I'll probably go and take some stuff over to Maurice[3]. I'll be really glad to see him!

Apart from that, I'm happy with my new life. Sometimes I do miss my Mum and little sister – but right now, France comes first.

Bye-bye, Mother, I'm writing you this from a café after leaving my truck for a while, and I've got to go, probably towards Belfort.

Your boy soldier,

Pierre

P.S. My mechanic knows Mr Bartolone from La Réole – so I feel quite at home.

Below is a letter from Augusta to Mrs. Barthe, referring to Pierre's correspondence above; it is indicative of the kind of woman Pierre's mother was.

20 August 1914

Dear Friend,

Your letters do me good; I don't lack courage, but sometimes black moods settle on me and make me shiver even though I try to drive them away.

Happily Pierre is living and acting like a soldier. He is under orders and can't go chasing after his fancies. He needs to be kept in check, or his impetuosity will make him try the impossible.

I've also had a long letter from him, by telegram from Dijon. That's their base, so they'll be back there from time to time. Yesterday I wrote to one of our friends who is a doctor in Dijon, so that we can communicate with Pierre via him and be sure to have all his news. The letters that come by the army postal service don't always get here.

He had been able to get off the camp for a while and wrote to me from a café: this is what he says: *(here she copies out the August 13th letter)* Like the note he sent you, this letter is full of energy and good spirit. It's obvious that he is quite happy. What would have become of him if he had been stuck here? He would have been bored stiff and no doubt been a nuisance to me!

This morning I got a letter from Louis *(her husband)* who seems to be happy with his situation. When his work for the day is finished he goes off on long rides with his friends. The money he took, plus his army pay, should be plenty for him. He doesn't seem to worry much about money, and has bought, for goodness' sake, a fine English saddle! He wants me to send him some clothes, because the weather is getting colder. It is difficult to send parcels, especially by express post, so I advised him to buy a big officer's greatcoat.

Is Mr Barthe equipped to face the cold?

Do you know what Louis suggested? I can't believe that at such a difficult time as this he gives so little thought to the future. He has suggested that I go and join him up there. 'The fare is only 46 francs', he says: 'I've got enough to pay for it, and all the fellows are getting their wives to join them. I'd like you to come as well'. He hasn't thought it through, the poor dear! What do you think? I'm sure your husband hasn't suggested such a thing to you. My husband is so placid that he seems completely unaffected by the great matters which are taking place; whereas, like all good Frenchmen, he should have a heavy heart. Perhaps if he knew that Pierre has gone off to war he would be a bit

---

3   Pierre and Maurice, a cousin of the former, were approximately the same age and close friends.

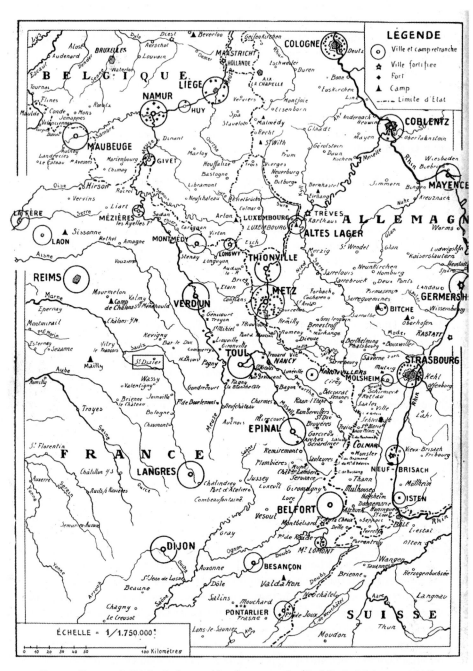

Eastern France: St Dizier is denoted by the rectangle. (*Le Miroir*, 16 August 1914).

more worried, but I haven't told him.

Bad news this morning. The Germans have reached Brussels. It would be good if we could floor them all with a single blow. They will make our soldiers suffer, and the rest of us as well before it's over. We must be confident: we shall never be beaten. Today's news has really upset me and I can't cope with it.

I have sent Louis' address to Mr. Barthe. I'll be happy if they see each other. My father is working very hard to cover Louis' absence. He never stops. Mr. Bonnat, a friend, has volunteered to help us with the car. I'm afraid we're rather taking advantage of him. At the moment everyone is rallying round and helping us.

Our very best wishes to you all – Paulette and I send you our love.

Augusta Suberviolle

Below is a little note, written on a post card from Aisy-sur-Armançon, Cote d'Or dated 22 August 1914, a day on which the French lost more men than on any other day of the war when their Lorraine offensive was thrown back. The note seems a bit surreal in relation to that bad news. Pierre was evidently unaware of it, and the grandiose menu was designed to amuse and reassure his family.

Handwritten menu for a meal our cook served up during a long stop on the road:
Various hors d'oeuvre
Radish with salt
Barbels au gratin
Burgundy snails cooked in the Roussillon fashion
Veal à la Chambert Robert
Belgian salad
English cheese
Russian coffee
Japanese dessert
French biscuits

St Dizier, 25 August 1914
Dear Little Mum,

What a joy this morning when the post was given out and my name was called! I'd been waiting for news for a fortnight, and then this morning I got both the letter from the 18th and the telegram from the 21st. You can't imagine, Mum, how much good these letters did me! I am happy, it's true, but I quite often feel down.

Sunday, 23 August, 3 p.m. – taken from my diary. The church bells are ringing for evening service. I'm lying in a corner of the park where we are billeted, and I'm thinking of you, Mum: to think I only left you a fortnight ago. It seems such a long time without kissing you or teasing you. Your big lad is not unhappy, but what he misses is the affection you gave him at home. How much I value it now ! Often I get a ringing in my right ear, and say to myself "Mum is thinking about me".

I was writing that last Sunday, but the fact is, Mum, that everything's OK.

I am the youngest guy in the whole truck convoy. I am treated as a kid, as if I was their son. Everywhere I go, I am introduced as a 17 year old kid, and everyone shakes my hand warmly. We have been divided into groups for the cooking. In mine, there is Mr Malvy's secretary, two Deputy Prefects from the Gironde, a retired sailor, a man who has a garage in Toulouse, and a man who is a lawyer, the rest of them are mechanics who are very nice. They are a good bunch, with several well educated gentlemen. They all spoil me as the baby of the group: they give me the best bits of food at mealtimes, and a double ration of coffee and sweets if there are any. They are all very nice.

The food is OK. When we're camping out, the meals are fine: when we're on the road one of us has a snack of cheese and bread while the other is driving. I do my chores without batting an eyelid. I peel the potatoes like a proper housewife, and I cook like a cordon-bleu chef.

We've done some really hard runs, driving all day long. The dust is terrible, and you can't get rid of it, even with a brush. Everywhere we are made welcome, but that doesn't stop people ripping us off, so everything is expensive. I'm quite happy to be in the transport service, though it may not be quite as much fun in the winter.[4]

I was glad to see that all is fine at home. With a chauffeur who has the same skills as me, Grandpa is sure not to have any break downs[5]. So he can be proud of him.

I'm very pleased that all of you, dad, grandfather and you, have understood the way I feel. Your young man is French and wants to do his duty. Going away was just as hard for me as it was for you, believe me. You know how fond I am of you, so you will understand that I was a bit weepy when I heard the cattle-wagon door close on that Sunday night – who knows for how long? It was dark in there, with wooden benches and a smoky lantern. I stayed near the door, and there, sick at heart, I saw Montauban vanishing into the darkness. When I couldn't see it any longer, I felt very unhappy at the uncertain future ahead. Bit by bit I overcame those feelings, and now, when I think of Montauban, it gives me strength and courage. Yes I was sad, but I'm a cheerful young chap, and I was soon laughing again.

I'm pleased to hear about Dad's burst of patriotism: it will help him understand my feelings better.

Is my little Popo thinking of her big brother? I'd be glad to have a little note from her.

Bye-bye, Mum, big kisses for you, Paulette, grandfather and grandmother, and wish Dad happy birthday for me. Send me his address, and your photo as well as Paulette's and Dad's (I'm cross with myself for leaving them at home). Remember me to Rose, Godmother, Auntie, Barthe and my pals.

A kiss on your neck from your Little Pierre

BOOM, BOOM – that blasted cannon again!

War involving motor vehicles was something very new as we can see from this introduction to *Lectures pour tous* of 15 January 1915: *One of the notable things about the present war is the use in it of mechanical inventions and scientific processes. These have revolutionised tactics and strangely changed the face of battle. One of the most notable is the use of motor vehicles. Not only have they been invaluable for the movement and supply of the troops but they have also played an active role in the fighting and have become formidable war machines in their own right.* No doubt Pierre Suberviolle would have appreciated this vis-à-vis his military role.

---

4   His military identification book states he was in possession of a driver's license "for all gasoline vehicles" since 1913, delivered by the Préfet of Montauban.

5   His grandfather replaced Louis, called up in Brittany, at the veterinary practice.

Tringlots (French slang for truck drivers) ambushed by
German Uhlans (*Le Miroir*, 28 March 1915)

There are several letters from September and October, both from and to Pierre, who was making frequent trips between the base areas and the front line. He has no pressing money worries: *I don't smoke or drink wine any more, but it's not bothering me* (19 September). On 29 September he pointed out that he was now eighteen, and on 3 October came this to his father: *I'm at the front. The day before yesterday I was a hundred yards from the trenches when I heard bullets whizzing past me. Several of them hit the lorry, and by God they set my stomach churning. I was driving, so I couldn't shoot back, but I'm glad to say my mate did the necessary and felled the bloody Germans.*

It was to his little sister – evidently hoping that it would reach the attention of his parents – that he sent the first of several requests for money and warm clothes:

18 October 1914

My dear little Mimine, (*his sister Paulette*)

Many thanks for your long letter, which I really enjoyed. I got it yesterday evening at about eight o'clock. The postman found me with it while we were cooking a meal at the side of the road. I read it over and over again by the light of the fire while I was warming up the soup. It's been getting colder and foggy, and your letter warmed me up again. I read it ten times during the evening.

It was kind of you to tell me all about your class and everything that's going on at home and in Montauban. As for me I'm full of beans, but let me tell you this driving business isn't all fun. Since we left the Dijon base, I've been sent up to the northern section of the front, and do I know it? There's fog nearly all the time and freezing rain. I'm sure it's going to snow one of these mornings. It's a good thing I like cold weather and can cope with snow. We're with the English and they are good blokes. We drive them about and I can now even chat with them.

My job stays the same. We carry munitions, food supplies and soldiers, and are never idle. The other day I was driving about a mile and a half from the front line when WHIZZ – BANG! The earth erupted all round us as heavy artillery shells landed. The lorry was shaken by blast one, two and three times, each time with the WHIZZ before it. We just duck and wait. All of these ones overshot us and exploded harmlessly, leaving the lorry convoy safe and sound. Bombs from aeroplanes also do little harm unless they drop right on your head. You get used to them and now I don't take much notice of them. Shells can be raining down, and you just light your pipe and wait for the order to set off as if you were on peacetime manoeuvres.

To sum up it isn't the shellfire which bothers us but cold and hunger. We eat regularly, but we haven't been given warm things to wear. For a month now I've been wearing clogs to save on shoe leather. I'm not too bothered by the cold or damp. My shirt, pants and shoes are riddled with holes. Also I'd like you to send me a flannel shirt, my two Rasurel[6] jumpers, a pair of pants, a pair of socks, my muffler and a big pair of fur lined gloves. Send the parcel to the address in Dijon and they will send it on.

I had a letter from Dad the other day. What a lucky so and so to have ten days leave in Montauban! Enjoy your good luck, Dad!

Bother. I've got a duty to do! I'll go on with my letter later. I've got to go ten kilometres up to the front line to pick up wounded because my lorry is the fastest we've got.

Hugs and kisses, back in a minute.

This part of the letter is written carefully in ink; the following words were scrawled in pencil at the bottom of the page.

19 October. A couple of words – I'm in a hurry. I haven't had a penny since 15 September and it's now 20 October. Dad's at home so ask him to send me fifty francs by the ordinary post in a sealed envelope. By the time this gets to me I shall be in serious need of it, as I've just spent twenty francs on a leather jacket invaluable in the rain. Send it to me as fast as you can. I'll stop now as I have to go in ten minutes.

I can't wait to give you big kisses Paulette and Mum. I hope to give you a hug in a few months.

Your big brother, Pierre

4 November 1914 (*to his father – extract*)
... for the moment I'm off duty at Villers Cotteret while our lorries are being serviced. Our Renault at home is nothing compared with my fine 20 h.p. Delahay. It's a good little lorry which carries 2-3000 kilograms of load. It does 25 k.p.h. in convoy, but 50 k.p.h. when I'm on my own on a special mission. Whenever there's anything risky to do it's always me that's sent, and on the road my lorry is the fastest and always leads

---

6   Rasurel: A good quality but inexpensive underwear garment. [T's N]

Pierre Suberviolle at the wheel of his lorry. (Private collection)

the way. "Bring me some shovels and planks for trenching work" he says, and there I am with the bullets whistling about me. "Bring me some shells for the big guns", and there I am among the shell-bursts, not to mention the bloody German monoplanes trying to bomb us. They normally miss us by a hundred yards.

My Lieutenant is happy with me because I am resourceful and can understand maps, so he sends me off in the lead unsupervised.

Dad you can relax and laugh at the idea of me dressed in blue from head to foot with my hammer in my hand, and my face and hands smeared with grease, checking over all the parts of the lorry. I want to make sure that everything is working well, because the last thing you want is to break down in the line of fire with the bullets whizzing round you. The only problem I've had like that is a blocked fuel inlet, and then some dragoons guarded me while I cleared it with a piece of wire. Now I can teach you a bit about motor maintenance. I'm beginning to understand how everything on the lorry works. The servicing of the dirty drive chains is the worst thing I have to do.

4 November 1914 (*to Marie Antoinette Barthe – a brief note on a postcard, his only communication with her*)

Always happy to send news to friends. Just by sending these little scraps of paper home you gain a little more courage to face the challenges you meet every day. I'm sorry that not very much news reaches us. The other day I had a letter from Mr. Barthe full of patriotism and courage. However far away from the gunfire people are, they are

Augusta and Paulette Suberviolle. (Private collection)

all involved in some way in this horrible war which has already gone on too long. My sincere good wishes to your family, and to you in particular my affectionate regard.

Your trooper,

Suberviolle

Our shellfire goes on and on ...

6 November 1914

Dear Mum,

Be patient, as I must be myself. Don't upset yourself when you don't get any letters or only short ones. I have only received three of your letters since the start of the war, and I have to be patient: each day I'm waiting and nothing comes, although I know you write to me and write often. I send letters and cards to you as often as I can; do they all get through? There must be delays in the post.

Villers-Cotteret, 21 November 1914

Dear Mum,

If you only knew how happy I am! I've got the lovely photographs of you and my little sister. I have taken the trouble to show them to all the fellows and they all think you're both charming. They think you're twenty five and Paulette seventeen! It makes me feel very good to see them admiring your picture. Thanks also for the picture of Dad which completes the set of pictures of my dear family, made dearer in the four months I've been separated from you.

Thanks as well for the second parcel which arrived this morning. It was the one with the shirt, the pants and the splendid sheepskin gloves, and then in the bottom a bar of chocolate to spoil me. How can I be unhappy when everyone is thinking of me so much? Thank you too, little Paulette, for the socks which I found in the first parcel. They're the warmest I've ever worn and I never take them off. I've sent a note to Mrs. Duluc to thank her for the muffler. That dear lady doesn't forget me either.

I have also got the fifty franc money order, Mum, which topped off the joy I had in getting the photographs. I promise you I won't waste it and as soon it's cashed I'm going to buy a good pair of shoes and a good pair of boots. The Army doesn't provide them and I mostly go around in clogs. I think that's all I need for the moment, Mum, and I can look forward to any eventuality.

I'm not suffering too much from the cold, even though the thermometer has been at minus 5 for several days. I enjoy seeing the frost everywhere. Every morning the engines are frozen in spite of the straw we put on them and the anti-freeze we fill them with overnight, and it's quite a business getting them started. Once we're on the road it's a bit cold but quite fun driving on the icy surfaces. So you can see, Mum, that I'm still full of enthusiasm and courage, and I hope that these two qualities will last as long as it takes to wipe out these filthy Germans.

I've had a letter from Marie-Antoinette full of patriotism as usual. You can judge the pleasure I have in seeing that they are thinking of me even at Le Mas. I'm writing to Dad by the same post; he'll be happy to have a letter from me as well.

You know, Mum, you shouldn't go on at me about my beard. I'm continuing to shave it all except a little moustache because I want to keep looking smart even in wartime. Who knows if in Belgium or in Germany being well presented might go down well with the girls? Please excuse my youthful humour, Mum, I'm just happy to have your dear photos to hug.

Goodbye Mum, but I've forgotten to complain at you. What's this about you thinking I'd been killed? Do you really think I'm going to let the place I've lived in for eighteen years be taken by some Boche? If you write anything like that to me again I shall go red with rage and not write to you for a fortnight as a punishment, and a well-deserved one.

A big kiss on your neck from your big lad.

Pierre

P.S. Kisses to Paulette and good wishes to everybody.

Blast! The dinner is on fire! What bad luck, my beans are going to be burnt again. Too bad if they shout at me, because at least I've had the pleasure of writing to you.

15 December 1914

Dear Grandpa,

A couple of words because I'm very busy. Thanks for the money order, much appreciated because it will help me through Christmas Eve. Please send me my revolver without ammunition (you'll need to spin a yarn at the Post Office about it). You'll find it in the little square drawer in the shelf of the pokerwork table in my bedroom. Put it in its holster and an envelope wrapped up in towels and handkerchiefs. Send it as soon as you can because soon we're on the move from here.

Goodbye, Grandpa, with big kisses from your young soldier. Pass them on to Mum, Nini and Paulette.

Pierre

P.S. It's two o'clock in the morning and we've just got back. I've chosen to write now, because when the postman comes at five o'clock in the morning I shall be fast asleep rolled up in my blanket!

Villers-Cotteret, Christmas 1914
Dear Dad,

It's been a long time since I wrote to you. We've been through a tough time. We've only just now got back at four o'clock in the morning after a fortnight's uninterrupted driving, carrying shells and stakes – it's been amazing. I'm glad to say that the truck is still running well and the roads are dry (it's so cold it's cracking the stones!). The whole unit had our Christmas Eve party at 11 o'clock last night in an abandoned house, while the lorries were being unloaded. Marraine *(his Godmother)* had the bright idea of sending me a sausage, which we all shared. Then came a fine bottle of rum, which I had to pay for, out of my savings, being the youngest of the group. The others bought wine and cheese and stuff, so we had a nice little party, and when the half hour stop was over we got back on the road again and believe me we roared back to camp.

We've had some rough times but so far we haven't suffered a single hit. The Germans must be wild that they've fired all those shells at us without hurting anyone. We've been lucky to have been hidden by fog most of the time. It's still very cold, but I'm well, and I can tell you that my moustaches are now getting seriously long!

Are you pleased at having spent so much time with Mum with her dancing attendance on you? According to what she writes, you've had some really good times, and the worst of it is you then tell me about them to make my mouth water! I'm OK about it really, and happy that you had a good time.

Bye, Dad – I send you a kiss and although it's a bit early I send you my New Year wish: that we all meet again at home, victorious and in good health.

Your young soldier

Pierre

P.S. I hope you will pay my Christmas bonus with a money order. Put them in an ordinary envelope as this is the quickest way of paying what you owe me.

That same day, Pierre wrote his mother the same letter with this extra bit added:

Are you happy with the parcel? It's my Christmas bonus to you, so please take good care of it. The forage cap belonged to a Boche whose head I found, blown off by a shell! The cape belonged to the other Boche I despatched a few days ago. Tell Grandpa that one's for him! He should be happy to frame his medal with these two trophies of his grandson.

An undated letter from Vitry-le-François. It was more than likely written during autumn 1914 whilst Pierre conveyed munitions and supplies to the front. The letter, an almost illegible scribble, mentions how Pierre came by the German overcoat:

Dear Mr. Barthe,

I'm at Vitry, with four days of leave after four months of continuous slog, night and day. So you think I was bluffing? In spite of the enormous effort we've made and

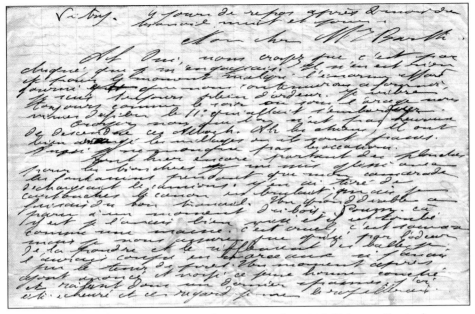

Pierre's letter posted from Vitry-le-François in late 1914. (Private collection)

are still making, we've nothing to show for it at the moment, but I'm still up for it. My spine is still tingling, as it did when we watched the 11th Division going up to the line on the night of the storm. Believe me that we are happy killing the Boches, after the terrible things the bastards have done in the villages they've passed through. I don't miss chances to get back at them.

The day before yesterday I was carrying a load of planks for trenches; I went and joined in with the infantry while my mate was unloading. I fired my gun until the barrel was hot, but I did a good job. A huge brute of a Boche suddenly appeared out of a clump of trees, but I saw him in time and 'BANG' – got him, and he went down like a sack of potatoes. Yes, it's cruel, and it's savage, but let me tell you that when you smell the cordite and hear the bullets whistling past it gets your dander up: I would have torn him limb from limb if I'd got hold of him.

A moment later we went forward, and I saw this young bloke lying on the ground gasping in his death agony. It made me feel sick, and I shall never forget the look in his eyes, but I was still enough of a barbarian to pinch his cape. I've sent it to my father as a good-luck token. The Boche material brings luck.

You can see I'm in good heart and ready to carry on. I had a letter from Le Mas which showed me the patriotism and bravery filling the hearts of those we have left behind. How can we not be brave when we think of our homeland and those with whom one day we will be reunited?

Goodbye, and Long Live France, Le Mas and Montauban! With sincere good wishes from the bottom of my heart,

Your boy soldier,

Pierre Suberviolle

My mother told me that he sent the same awful message to his mother and sister. On discovery of the letters in 1986, his widow Marie-Antoinette, shocked by the violence therein, destroyed them. Thus it is a bit of a mystery how this example survived.

From 9 to 19 of January, fierce fighting took place north of Soissons, which was repeatedly shelled by the Germans. Pierre posted a number of brief postcards from the vicinity:

25 January 1915
Dear Dad,

Excuse me for not writing for a few days, but we've been busy. You must have heard the newsflash from Soissons a few days ago. We nearly got captured. You can imagine what a pathetic figure I should cut sweeping the streets of Berlin! It wouldn't have come to that, as I have made up my mind to go on fighting right up to the end. In the end I got out of it, which is the important thing.

Nothing new in our work apart from that, except that we're fed up with the rain and mud. They've offered to make me a corporal, but I said no, as I'm happy with my lorry and my mates, and I think I'm too young to tell men of thirty and forty what to do.

Cheers, Dad, and big hugs.

Pierre

On the same day he wrote to his mother:

It was by a mere whisker that I avoided joining Maurice in Saxony[7]. We only just had time to turn the lorries round before the Boches opened fire on us from the windows of Soissons. I managed to get off a few shots in reply with my carbine, while my mate was scared shitless and clutching the steering wheel without daring to look back. It was there that I picked up the bag, the cartridges, the pot and a gun (I could only get the firing mechanism in the parcel). A fine set of New Year presents from your little trooper, don't you think?

I was also going to send you a helmet which I had hidden away (at the risk of two weeks in prison if anyone found out), but the bloke at the station noticed it, so it was goodbye, helmet. At least he kept his mouth shut!

Every day we go back to Soissons to retrieve stuff from the factories. The Boches have done a good job with their shelling, and most of the place is in ruins. We have had crazy good luck, with none of us being hit by shellfire as we go to and fro. The other day I was loading the lorry with shells when a bomb from an aeroplane fell right by me. It was in perfect condition because it hadn't gone off. The officer asked me to give it to him, and he's a good bloke, so I couldn't refuse ...

15 February 1915
Dear Mum,

It's midnight, black dark and pouring with rain. I'm taking advantage of a couple of hours of guard duty to get you up to date. You've no idea how much I enjoyed reading your last letter. It shows that you are busy and brave. When I read your letter believe

---

7   His cousin had apparently been taken prisoner.

A convoy near the front line. (*Le Miroir*, 15 August 1915)

me, it did me a lot of good ... Then a word from my Mum (and you know your big boy can understand you), so thanks for your long letter and a kiss on the neck and I go on:

We find ourselves in a quiet period – perhaps too quiet. Our lorries are much the same, but I can't give you any details because the censor doesn't allow it. What I can tell you is that my lorry is still running well, and the roads are still dreadful. The weather is mucking us about as well, continually drenching us and storing up rheumatism for our old age!

My health is actually good, and since you ask I haven't got a single thing wrong with me – no illness and no injury. I'm so well the lads in the platoon have nicknamed me 'Brains'. I am in good spirits. Even in the most boring moments I am enthusiastic and cheerful. A few jokes with the old blokes (between 20 and 40) and they laugh again ! That's another reason why they call me the Brains of the platoon. Sometimes, though, I get the blues, and who wouldn't in this bloody awful weather? Then I get up on the lorry, fill up my pipe and spend an hour or so just looking at the photos of you and Paulette without worrying about anything else. Then I think about my old life, and again I think of you, Paulette, Granny and Grandpa and our friends: the house, Montauban and Toulouse are all turning fuzzy in my memory. I give you a kiss on the neck and pass on to another page ...

The war is making us less human. We are transformed into machines fixed in our roles, stopping and going according to orders, and always in line behind the officer. On we go on the filthy roads and under the shellfire, wherever we must. We become hardened to the horrors in quite a shocking way. We don't worry about anything, and you must imagine me lighting up a cigarette while the shells are falling all round, as calm and collected as after dinner at home. (Perhaps I should say calmer, as Grandpa's wrath is more frightening than the shells! – tell him I'm only joking).

Pierre on potato peeling duty. (Private collection)

I would sum it up by saying that the longer it goes on the more fatalist we get. When I come home you won't recognise me, though there's one thing that hasn't changed: when the chief gives me an order I moan about it, but he laughs because he knows that in the end I'll do it. You might be interested that although I generally get on well with everybody, I have struck up a friendship with the medical orderly, who was a medical student in Toulouse. He's very considerate, and we share memories of our times at the university.

So everything's OK and we can pass on to practical details. Thank you, Mum, for the last parcel with the socks and the tin of jellied meat. We feasted on that, I can tell you. I've got five parcels, so there's just one still to come. I've got the one with the famous gloves and the belt. Could you write to Mrs. Noby to thank her. I have already written to her thanking her for the belt.

You mentioned the money order which you're going to send. I'll be glad when it arrives, because Granny's present didn't amount to much and I'm so skint that I have to drink water instead of wine. Just send an ordinary money order by recorded delivery. As to Grandpa's fine presents, could you send me those, too? I wasn't there at New Year to find the usual splendid bank note under my plate! Whatever it is it won't be too much, as I've got lots to do washing everything, getting the oil and grease out, and doing all the mending and darning. I look like a slob and I know a nice old lady who will do my cleaning for me.

Thanks little Mum for having looked after my business, and I'm sure you take as much care with it as I would. I don't think there'll be another stop tonight because we're doing a round trip.

Big hugs for you and everyone, and a special kiss on the neck for you.

Pierre

Say nice things to Philomena and her lad, and tell him that I shall be glad to have him to help me with the cooking. Shake the brave Belgians by the hand. I'm glad to hear they're happy in the house.

3 March 1915
A card with accompanying photo

My cap at a jaunty angle, with a smile on my face, here I am peeling potatoes. You can see Little Mum, that I'm still well.

Some short letters in March: Pierre requires money and complains of postal service irregularities.

28 March 1915
Dear Little Mum,

I'm so glad to have rejoined the unit. I read and re-read your two last letters, which made me smile. I've been to the post office with your money order which arrived well on time.

Let me start at the beginning. Eight days ago I left the unit to go to a big town in the rear to collect a new lorry. One of the reasons I refused to be made up to corporal was the danger that I would be sent to a vehicle depot in a base area and spend the rest of the war far away from the Boches. I want to fight this war right to the end, and that's what I'm going to do.

The Lieutenant wanted to do something for me to show his confidence in me, and he has just given me a superb truck which is virtually new. It's not a light one of around 30 h.p., but a great big 50 h.p. monster I'm driving at the moment. It's harder to drive and maintain than my old lorry, but at last I've got something which flies along and will see me through the rest of the war without a problem.

I'm happier with that than with stripes on my arm, because it shows that they have recognised that although I'm young I've got a serious outlook on things, and can be relied on to drive this fine machine and bring it through safely. I'm sure you will be glad to hear that and will not regret putting so much into bringing your son up.

Now I need to explain about the 100 francs: I tell you the truth as I would to an older sister. Dad is very kind and he sends me 20 francs from time to time. I can't say the same about Grandpa. Compared with the amount he used to give me every year without my even asking, I've only had 25 francs. Does he think he should forget me now I'm at war?

Anyway, the day I went to get the new lorry I was flat broke. It's a big town far from the fighting, so I borrowed 50 francs from one of the fellows (he was a parliamentary candidate and a sub-prefect, and he was very happy to lend it to me). For eight days I had the pleasure of sleeping in a proper bed, and it was the first time for seven months

Pierre's photograph of Champagne peasant woman posing with Poilu in traditional headdress. (Private collection)

Undated comic photo taken by Pierre of faked motor accident. (Private collection)

that I'd taken my clothes off to go to bed! I ate in restaurants again a bit like when I was a student. I hope you agree that I deserved a bit of a break after seven months at the front.

I can see you starting to smile! This is where the money went:

Washing and ironing all my things 5F.

Leggings to soften the discomfort of my worn-out boots 5F.

Planks and tools I need to sort out the new lorry 10F.

Odds and ends, writing paper, envelopes and so on 10F.

That left 20 francs for wine, tins of food and other daily expenses. You can see I'm not living it up like an officer, or gadding about, and spend the money you send me wisely.

You tell me not to tire myself out. I'm with you, but the work is there to do. You can see from the photo that I'm getting on fine, and I don't have any sleepless nights. The main thing is that I keep being lucky . The other day one of my mates got hit in the foot by a shell and another got hit in the arm. It was no big deal, and I even dressed his wounds as if I was a medical student.

Now Mum, let's speak of you. Have you got round to choosing your new suit? I'm sure that you have and that Dad will be delighted to have his little wife with him.

Good bye, Mum. Big hugs to you and everyone else.

Pierrot, your trooper.

Each letter has a distinct content style: When writing to his grandfather, Pierre's style is that of a fierce warrior thirsting for revenge; to his Father he speaks of mechanical things; sentimentality is evident when corresponding with his mother. In the following correspondence he adopts a gentle and florid style with his sister.

20 April 1915

My dear little Popo

How lovely of you to send me this kind letter. You've no idea how much I enjoyed reading it. I can see from the way you write that my little Popo is becoming a big girl. I shan't be able to recognise you when I come home but it will be really nice to hug you again. With your pretty little face and your long blonde hair you were really cute when I left home, but I'm sure you'll be even more beautiful when I come home as I am always hoping that I will.

To thank you for your letter I've sent you a little parcel. In it you will find a headdress of the style that the peasant girls wear here in Champagne. You have to fix the slide to the border at the front. They call it a Bagnolet, and all the women wear them when they are working in the vines. I think you'll like to wear it in the garden: I've chosen a pink one because I know pink suits you so well. In the parcel you'll also find a pen holder which I made out of two German bullets. I hope you'll like these presents and will send me a letter in return.

At the moment we're back at a repair facility for maintenance to be done on the older vehicles in the squadron. After that who knows where we shall be sent? I don't know. All is calm at the moment, so the war is not much in our thoughts, and I can tell you that time is starting to drag, we just have to grit our teeth and carry on to the end.

Lots of hugs and kisses.

Pierre

2

On the banks of the Ypres Canal

1915

10 April: French offensive on the banks of the Meuse succeeds in capturing Les Eparges Ridge, which the Germans have held since September 1914.

22 April: Second Battle of Ypres opens with German use of poison gas.

23 September-6 October: Franco-British offensives in Champagne and Artois.

1 October: Anglo-French landings at Salonika.

5 October: Bulgaria enters the war on the side of the Central Powers.

6 October: Serbia invaded and overrun by Central Powers.

3 May 1915 – Vicinity of Dunkirk

Dear Mum and Dad,

It's 8.00 at night and drizzling. The sea mist has risen right up to the edge of my dugout, so I'm alone and better able to chat to you.

Yes, Mum, it's a big hole I've dug for myself in a dune facing the sea. It's where I'm going to sleep as long as we stay here. It's not particularly warm and some might think it a strange place to shelter, but what a view! With that, each evening and your letters, my spirits are much revived. When I look out over the sea I am struck by the contrast between the immensity of nature compared with my own insignificance: it makes me think of the war, with its brave deeds mingled with barbarous ones.

Every evening at about 7.00 a Taube[1] flies over the harbour and the town, making various signals with different coloured lights. Then it drops a few bombs and flies off followed by our anti-aircraft and machine gun fire. About ten minutes then pass, during which the people of the town come out to hide among the dunes, because they know what's coming: then WHIZZ – BANG – the shells arrive from an unseen cannon! The ground shakes under the bombardment, and the explosions spread death and destruction wherever they land. I've never heard such powerful detonations before, and it may well be that the papers are right in saying that the Germans are using a 380mm gun. You can imagine the terror of the townspeople who have never been under fire before. For three days they haven't been able to live a normal life. Then, as night falls, the guns cease firing one by one, and then the green lights of the torpedo boats criss cross the darkness, and the searchlights on the fort probe the horizon and the sky.

And so then, when everything is quiet again, and the sea breeze blows into my

---

1   Rumpler Taube: Early German monoplane (1910) with wings resembling that of a pigeon or dove.

42

mole-hole, I roll myself up in my blanket, light my pipe and wait for sleep to take me away from these daydreams which in spite of myself rise up out of the waters.

I think I can be excused a short period of moping after nine months on campaign, but in fact low spirits affect me only when we are far from the fighting; they soon disappear when we get close to the dirty Boches again. Here in this great port, right on the border of France just a stone's throw away from Belgium, I've regained my spirits and my urge to get involved again.

Lastly Mum and Dad, thanks very much for the last money order. During my nine months of wandering I have almost always had to pay for my meals (the lorry with the food supplies crashed on a tree). The money has come in handy and don't think I waste any of it. Even if I wanted to I have not had the opportunity.

Goodbye my lieutenant with a big hug, and goodbye little Mum I give you a big hug too. Your little boy is still full of beans.

Pierre

Most of this letter was published under the heading "Letter of a Montauban soldier", anonymously except for PIERRE at the bottom, in the local newspaper *L'Indépendant du Tarn-et-Garonne* on 5 June 1915.

In May and June Pierre sends several postcards and short letters from Belgium, written in brief moments in between his incessant frequent journeys along the road.

6 June 1915 (*to his sister*)

... It is true that we have some moments of spare time and this is usually in the evening when the weather is good and we have finished our work. It is then that I take a little dip in the sea. Do you remember little Popo when we used to go swimming in the Tarn, and I used to make you drink the dirty water? This swimming is now the only leisure activity left to me. After a long, dangerous and tiring day it is a real pleasure to throw yourself into the fine North Sea.

1 June 1915

Thanks dad for the parcel with all the little useful things, which I am very glad to have. Thanks also for the photos. You look like a real conquering hero with your curly moustache, your neat goatee beard along with a fine looking wife and a superb dog. You are a true officer, upholding the fame of the French army. Big hugs.

Pierre

7 July 1915

From Desvres-Lumbres, near Boulogne

Dear little Mum,

I am sorry that you have not heard from me in a few days. Hug me because I really have not had a minute. Here we are in the rear. What a paradise it is, Mum, if only you knew. We left Malo above Dunkirk on the 4th and from there we were sent to Saint-Omer and then Desvres, which is outside the battle zone. What a relief to be driving on good French roads. Belgium is fine but it is nothing compared to our beautiful France. It is the first time that I have felt moved by the sight of my own country. Don't laugh, Mum, but if I had lived through these times when I had to take those old school

Louis and Augusta Suberviolle with Loko. (Private collection)

exams, I surely would have had better grades, don't you think? I think I become a boy again when I leave the frontline. I am so, so peaceful and a sense of well-being and security enfolds me in spite of myself. We are already in the twelfth month of the war and here I can sleep easy without worrying about shells or anything. It is not that their bombs bother us a lot, but this peace makes you think you are in paradise. From every house the people smile out at us; it is the first time they have seen soldiers here and everyone is happy to see the French troops coming up to the front. They ask us all sorts of questions and we are glad to reply to these brave people, who have all got someone at the front. Some of them even insist on hugging and kissing us, which makes us smile but we submit with a good grace. Sadly this is not going to last beyond the day after tomorrow. We have come here to get enormous trunks of pine wood to provide platforms for huge English guns, and we will be going back to the front more cheerful than before because we have had this encouraging welcome from the people.

As for the English, the war is finishing off my education. When we are in the rear of the English army it is the English we deal with. Since I am the only person in the squadron who has any idea of English (and I have astonished myself with how much I remember from school) I have been acting as an interpreter for the last 5 or 6 days so that my lieutenant can communicate with the English officers and sometimes give orders. This is great fun I assure you, and the more I do it the better I get. Now it is just 2 more days and we will be back with the Belgians, and my Flemish isn't up to much. I just put on a northern accent and I feel as if I spoke several languages here!

Now let's talk about something even more interesting. There is a rumour that they are going to give all the soldiers at the front 8 days leave. Everyone will take his turn in order of age. In my unit as soon as we have got back to Dunkirk two men will go off on leave, and then two more after eight days and so on. As I am the youngest it will take two or three months before it gets round to me ...

I can see what's going to happen: the men coming out of the line are surely going to start mucking about because there is no prospect of punishment, then they'll be late back, and then no doubt the army will cancel the privilege. That is what I fear, and then I'll have to wait for another 4 months, which is too long. If I have to stick that, I will but is there any way of getting around it? I remember that when you were worried that I would be put in the infantry, you found a way of getting to see the commanding officer and persuading him to put me somewhere else. Can you find some excuse to write to my officer to fix it so my turn comes more quickly?

If there is a way, I am sure that you will be as happy as I will for us to meet up as soon as possible. Have a go and if it doesn't work I shall have to be patient. From here we are off to the front and where shall we be in 4 months? Will we be able to keep writing to each other?

Goodbye little Mum.

Big hugs to you and everyone at home.

Pierre

At this point in the text appear a number of Pierre's photographs (see below) that cannot be dated more precisely than autumn/winter 1914 and spring/summer 1915.

4 August 1915 (*to Antonin Barthe*)

I am writing to you from the banks of the Ypres canal. Yesterday while we were driving through the woods with some concrete for the English trenches, we ran into some poison gas, which is quite a common thing around here. I had already used my gas mask and I hadn't remembered to replace the bottle of hyposulphite to soak the pad in. It didn't work and I found myself red in the face and coughing my guts up. Happily we were driving towards the rear, and we were soon out of the gas cloud. I really don't want to die choking like that: a bullet, well that is war, but gas is something else. Today my companion and I are still unwell, and I have a splitting headache. I decided that the

Poilus outside improvised shelters. (Private collection)

British Tommies and French *Poilus* fraternize at a railway yard. (Private collection)

Column of Tommies on the march in Flanders. (Private collection)

best thing to do is to unburden myself by chatting a bit to you. Between you and me I think I am on the mend, and I am sure that by tomorrow I will be okay. Don't mention this to my family because they will upset themselves for nothing.

7 August 1915

It is now a whole year since I became a soldier. It seems a long time, but you get used to everything after a time. It is only my clothes which are giving me a problem. Dear little Mum can you please send me as quickly as possible:

- 2 well-made flannel shirts of a dark colour
- 2 woollen gaiters (I can't stick the canvas ones)
- 1 pair of braces
- 6 coloured peasant handkerchiefs
- 3 bath towels
- 1 sweater
- 1 pair of large sheepskin gloves

In a word a new set of kit. I will send you what is left of the old ones so you can

"Sending troop parcels". Drawing by Louis Suberviolle. (Private collection)

see what a state they are in. Could you also add a good sponge, some shaving soap and 2 bars of soap?

21 August 1915 (*to his mother*)

The other day I had a little disaster. I lost my wallet with all its contents. Could you ask Grandpa to send me another military pass book or a duplicate as quick as you can. If anything happens to me I have got nothing to identify myself. Can you also send me as quick as you can a photo of you and Popo (who according to Dad is turning into a charming young lady).

And there is one other thing that is bothering me. With the wallet I lost 75 francs which I was keeping for emergencies (that is your 50 and 25 I got from Dad). I have only got 40 pence left in my money box and I've lived on that for 6 days. For the moment I have only got 4 pence, just enough to pay for a single beer when I am thirsty. I have often had a very dry throat in these recent days especially when it has been hot, and without a penny I couldn't have a drink. Happily we have just been issued with 2 litres of wine which will keep me going for 4 days. After that who knows?

Hugs etc

Pierre

27 August 1915

Dear little Mum

Today I got another letter from you which was a pleasure as usual, especially when I found out you were completely better. Take care not to overdo things because my heart

The "squad". (Photo by Pierre Suberviolle, private collection)

is too full to think that you are ill. Have a big hug and we won't talk about it anymore.

You are going to make me overproud if you call me the kindest boy in the world (when I want ...). I was very happy to meet here plenty of clients all thinking very kindly of me[2], remembering "Suberviolle's son". The first who recognised me was one called Cambo, Mr Constant's servant and then straight away another came to shake my hand. They all recognised me straight away and I knew who they were ... even though I had never seen them before. But that's what they were expecting. They were all very impressed when I said to them that I remembered their farm very well because I had often been there with Dad. They were also pleased to see me just as filthy and disgusting as they were, because here in the war zone we don't like people who put on airs. It is true that my beard is not as big as theirs but I like to have a small one under control, a neat little parting in my hair and I like to be properly shaved. This is the only aspect of pride in my appearance which I have kept up with, in imitation of the English. They recognised that there was something special about me, because they called me "Monsieur" in a grand way, something which I didn't really welcome because just plain Suberviolle is perfectly all right. We had a couple of beers together and everybody was happy. It was on this leave that I asked if they would load the lorries every evening and after that we took the stuff up to the second line of trenches in complete darkness. They all shook my hand and wished me good luck and above all not to bash myself up.

And so I lived a week with these squaddies, still recognisably southern in spite of their time in the north.

It must be a real pain dealing with all the little domestic chores that you have; maids who can't cook and force you to become a cordon-bleu yourself and drivers who don't know how to drive. Be patient, Mum, and with good will they will get there in the end. I have had a similar experience this end which doesn't stop me from smiling at all the troubles that women get into, especially when I am reading about them with cannon fire in my ears.

Something else that interests me is to know that my little Popo is turning into a

2   Pierre is referring to his family's veterinary practice clientele.

big girl, a young lady and almost a woman because she is already starting to tease me a bit. I don't mind her pinching some of my rice powder but rouge? No! Tell her that her lips must be pretty enough to wait a bit before she needs to use lipstick. I really like to see her with little blue and white outfit, her white stockings and shoes and above all her lovely blonde hair and her eyes like the Virgin Mary. I can tell you that if I was there I'd give her such a big hug that I would make you jealous.

As for Grandpa, I am happy to see that he has not changed at all. He is match-making again, for Marc this time. I am sure he is going to excel himself and choose a kind and pretty little girl who will make a lovely home. Isn't it right Monsieur Viguier, can we trust your good taste? My dear Grandpa goes on being young in body and mind. I should be just as happy as him, because thanks to him my own future, God willing, will be just as good as his.

Now about poor Dad, who has had the unfortunate idea to fall down. I couldn't help smiling because that is Dad all over. Everyone has his own way of doing things, Mum. I think that the war is now lasting too long for him and so he is bored and he is not following his diet. I can understand that but I am sure that when you are up there with him (and make sure you stay as long as you can), he will see reason, dreaming about his pretty daughter (about whom he gets very excited when he is writing to me) and his son, who has been eyeball to eyeball with these dirty Boches for more than a year now.

Hugs and kisses for all the family.

Pierre

In September Pierre sent rings to all the members of the family, which he had made himself out of things he found lying around. A little note accompanied each ring:

September 1915
Dear Dad,

At last I have finished your ring, which I made out of the fuse of a 77 millimetre shell, which fell a few yards away from the lorry at the Blue Farm on the banks of the Yser. I did everything with a knife and polished on wood. Although it isn't brilliantly done you can see that I am starting to have the skills of a jeweller. It has taken me a month to make it. Get your initials engraved on it and if it is too small you can easily get it made bigger. I hope you like it Dad, because here we think it brings good luck.

P.S. Could you send me a money order as soon as possible, as I have just lost my wallet with all my spare money in it.

Dear Mum,

Here is a ring for you; it is one of the most recent that I have made and took me a long time. It came from a Boche shell which fell on Ypres in the Yser department. I have fixed a French centime into it. Don't you think that is original? I hope you like it and will be pleased to have a souvenir made by your big lad.

Dear Mademoiselle Paulette,

I made your ring in March when I was in the Aisne department. I did it all with my knife and you can see how I am gaining skill with it. I made it out of the fuse of

---

LES
BIJOUX DES POILUS

IL nous paraît intéressant de signaler à l'attention de nos Lecteurs, l'initiative bien française, prise par une Maison de Bijouterie parisienne, plus que centenaire.

Au profit de nos Soldats, elle a installé dans ses vitrines, une Exposition d'objets exclusivement exécutés sur le front, et se fait leur intermédiaire pour en propager la vente dont le produit est intégralement envoyé au bénéficiaire.

L'indication des nom et adresse des Soldats prouve l'authenticité de ces souvenirs de guerre, tous intéressants par la variété et la valeur de leur inspiration.

Si les " BIJOUX DES POILUS " vous intéressent, en vous adressant à la " GERBE d'OR ", 86, rue de Rivoli, Paris, vous aurez un vrai souvenir de guerre et vous ferez une bonne action.

A contemporary advertisement to sell jewellery made by soldiers:
SOLDIERS' JEWELLERY – We draw readers' attention to a patriotic initiative taken by a Paris Jeweller with a hundred years' experience in the business. To raise money for the troops it has mounted an exhibition of pieces of jewellery made by serving soldiers at the front. All the money raised is posted to the soldier concerned. (*Annales*, 12 December 1915)

a German shell which fell on Soissons. I didn't send it to you sooner because I didn't want Mum to be jealous. Are you happy with it girlie? I have spent a long time on it I can assure you but because it was for you nothing was impossible.

Pierre also posted a second ring to his beloved grandmother, Nini.

Monday, 20 September 1915
Dear Mum,

Thanks for your card which I got yesterday and specially for the pâté you sent the other day. Yesterday I was on the road and had nothing to eat, I dipped into my little reserve and to the astonishment of my comrades I produced the great big box and with my pals in the squadron we all polished off this little dinner provided by the house of Viguier-Suberviolle:

Hors d'oeuvre: sausage
Main course: 2 enormous slices of pâté
Dessert: chocolate
Thanks, Mum, on behalf of myself and all the lads here.
Yesterday I had a nasty experience: I was soldering one of the engine pipes when I

burnt off my little moustache! What a tragedy when I had put so much into growing it! And now here I am looking like a 17 year old new recruit just like I was a year ago! I thought I would look young again, but in fact I've gone all serious like a big boy (one who in nine days will be 19!)

So my 18th year has been spent at war, and I've not seen you once. Here I am 19, and still far from you. Could you please send me the 50 francs (from Marraine), as I have to buy the boys a drink: as the youngest it is expected of me, and they all look after me so well.

Pierre

23 September 1915

I'll be home in four or five days!

Pierre

At last, Pierre managed to obtain home leave where he subsequently spent his 19th birthday. Back at the front, he recounted the return journey.

Friday 8 October 1915

Just got five minutes to chat with you, little Mum, first of all about the journey. I made sure to fill my pipe as soon as I was in the wagon and en route for the front. I was feeling very down, and there's no point denying it, but I consoled myself with the thought of taking up my rambling Gypsy life style again. There's also the fact that there is a job to do, and one might as well do it cheerfully. When you get near the fighting again you recover your sense of patriotism, which is rather dulled by home life.

Anyway, it was Sunday night at about quarter to five when the train for the returnees from leave set off for the north, and I had a big lump in my throat when the branches of the trees hid Montauban from me (how long for this time, I wonder?) I had to wipe a tear from my eyes. I felt the need to wave my kepi out of the window as if I was saying goodbye to an old friend! The train trundled along slowly but remorselessly. At the regulation 25 k.p.h. it took an age, and it wasn't until 10 p.m. that we got to Cahors. We were at Brive at three in the morning and at Limoges at mid-day on Monday.

I was alone in the compartment, and thanks to my haversack stuffed full of good things and my trusty flask, the night passed quite well. After that the time weighed heavily, when the crying need was to hurry up to get to grips with the bloody Boches again.

Finally I got off at Limoges, none the worse for wear, with my haversack, my flask, my bundle, my pipe in my mouth and my kepi at a jaunty angle. In fifteen minutes the Paris express was due. If anyone gets in my way? – bugger it! But without much difficulty I made it on to the express, and soon we were flying along: we were at the Gare d'Austerlitz[3] by eight.

It was the first time I'd been in Paris on my own. It presented problems: how would I make out without looking like a country bumpkin? I summoned up the courage to get out of the station, I checked myself over – my old kepi on my head, with a world weary air and my shoulders hunched up, I went through the barrier muttering 'On leave from

---

3   Gare d'Austerlitz: One of the main Paris rail stations, named after Napoleon's great 1805 victory. The reader will note the length of Pierre's journey – 27 hours; it takes approximately six hours today. [T's N]

the Front'. 'Pass' said the ticket collector, and in three measured steps I was free! In three more steps I found myself in the big boulevard outside.

At first I just stood there, flabbergasted. The pavement was a mad scramble, and in the street a dizzying procession of trams, taxis, cars and lorries. There was no way that I was going to be able to walk to the Gare du Nord as I'd hoped. It was more terrifying to think of crossing a Paris street than to go among the shellfire at the front, so I hailed a taxi in my best Parisian accent, and away we went to the Gare du Nord. I was stunned by all the great boulevards and the crush, and more than once I had to cling on to the side of the taxi. In the end we made it to the Gare du Nord, where the express for Dunkirk wasn't due to leave till midnight.

So I found myself in Paris with four hours to kill. I found a Bouillon-Chartier[4] where I had a feast for three francs. Imagine, Mum! There I was with my hair all over the place and my face and hands none too clean, and in front of me my kit in a heap, with my haversack, greatcoat, and my flask, with my old kepi on the top. They weren't very good company, but they caught people's attention, and I heard them whispering "Goodness! He's from the Front but he doesn't look old enough to be a soldier!" With all these admiring glances I soon found myself sitting in front of a little table with a white tablecloth, adorned with a vase (just how you know I like it) with a bunch of jasmine and a velvety red rose. At the table on my left there sat a veteran of the 1870 war; as I took my seat he saluted me respectfully, and I saluted him back as best I could. On my right were three young people and a young man (reformed, I expect) who was a complete phony. One of the girls was nothing much, but the other two were charming, typically chic Parisians with that indefinable air they have. They greeted me warmly as well; when you come from the Front everyone is your friend.

It was in this pleasant environment that I ate my first meal in Paris without a care in the world. Then, leaving my bundle and flask, but keeping my old cap and my haversack, I went for a wander round.

It was ten o'clock, and I found myself, pipe in mouth and hands in pockets, on one of the great boulevards; I decided to take a gamble and cross the street. How did I do it? No idea! I just strolled over to the central pavement under the streetlamp, and from there I strolled over to the other side. I proved that crossing the road is not a major feat of exploration, and I'm getting as nimble as a Parisian. I got quite a taste for it, and crossed and recrossed several times just for the fun of it. I'm not saying everything that I saw or everywhere I went, but at quarter to midnight I was on time at the Gare du Nord, and made it on to the train without a problem.

We got to Dunkirk at three in the afternoon of Wednesday, and I went straight to the front. It didn't take long to find everything as I remembered it; I even enjoyed the sound of the guns! Here everything happens so fast that you don't have time to get miserable.

Quick, quick – Bye for now, as it's time to get going. Big hugs, stay well and wise and write to me often. Big hugs for Popo and Grandma and Grandpa.

P.S. don't forget the two parcels– one for Grenier, and one for my mates here (10 of them) – it's a tradition for anyone returning from leave!

PIERRE

---

4   A cheap restaurant, of which there are many in Paris today.

Pierre's "eating irons". Photograph by D. Labaume. (Private collection)

19 October 1915

Dear Little Mum,

Where's that nice little table in the Parisian restaurant now? A passing dream and a fancy, which left me high on life and fun. And here I am back at the wooden table on whose top I carved my name, eating off an aluminium plate with a bendy fork! I derive a certain amount of pleasure from being back here, filthy and stroppy like an old soldier. I love to smoke the pipe I had when I was a student, my faithful friend: every time I fill it it reminds me of my time on leave, whether at Montauban or at Toulouse. Now it's back at war with me, and who knows what it will see in the times to come? Whatever may befall I'm sure the pipe will carry with it the memories of this terrible time.

Dammit, it's here and now! But the top and bottom of it is that I've slipped back into my old ways. I had a good eight hours' sleep. For a week I was far too posh for a soldier but that's all over, and I've started to swear and shout again as one must here. Everything's back to normal.

9 November 1915 (*to Paulette*)

Dear little mistress of the house,

You sent me such a lovely letter that I owe you a long reply. I will give you all the news so that Granma and Grandpa can enjoy it as well. I am assuming that Mum has gone to Brest.

But, Miss, you should leave off harassing your big brother. What's all this meddling in my future affairs? At least you do it so nicely that I haven't the heart to go on at you about it. Away with your mischief!

The main thing here is that winter is coming on fast. Every day we have rain or thick morning mists, which are blown away by biting winds which freeze all the water. It's not a bundle of laughs, I can assure you. It is as cold and damp here as in the middle of winter at home. It's a filthy place and we shall end up freezing to death here. It's not a patch on the good bed in my little bedroom, and I often shiver under the basic bed cover we have here. It's true that for a while now we have grown thicker skins, and will be able to get through this second winter. It's not fun, but if it has to be gone through to win the war, so be it.

Dear Popo, will you do something for me? Please ask Grandpa for some money, as I need to buy a sailor's waterproof to keep the rain off. They're about 30 francs, I think. When I was on the road the other day my wet cape froze solid like a shell, and if I hadn't had to move them all the time my arms would have frozen stiff as well. It was unpleasant, and showed that I need something waterproof. I'm sure that you will do that for your big brother.

Thanks Popo for being so sensible. Keep doing your homework, but find time to write often to your big brother.

Big hugs to you and Granny and Grandpa.

Pierre wrote to his parents that same day:

The worst thing is the mud: you sink into it and get stuck, and it freezes your feet. It's a real pain driving in such weather and on such roads, and with it going dark so early. I need a couple of things which I'm sure you'll send: first of all some folding scissors, and an electric torch to go in my pocket for when I have a breakdown at night. I'll need a few spare batteries as well. Round here they are charging 15 francs each for batteries, when you can normally get them for about three francs each. Then I also need a pair of leather leggings without straps, the old ones I brought with me from Montauban are quite worn out.

There was a fourth item on Pierre's list, but the paper is torn!

You're going to say that I'm very demanding, but you might see it my way if you knew how unappealing the prospect of another winter is. Let's hope it passes quickly and we are soon victorious.

Big hugs
Pierre

Saturday 14 November 1915
Dear Mum and Dad,

At last you are together again, which will be a joy to you both. I can imagine you starting off on a second honeymoon. You're alone in the house, and you don't see many people. You cook your own meals, and your canoodling goes on all day! But I can't go on at you or my lieutenant will give me eight days' extra duty. (= a punishment)

I've got plenty of news for you: you know I've got a new lorry. It's because of a blunder made by one of my mates who, while I was away, drove my lorry into a shell hole and broke the wheels, axles and springs! When I got back the vehicle was still under repair. Would it ever come back? Often they put lorries back in different units, so to avoid ending up being stranded who knows where I took one of the old lorries which had only one driver. For a month I was stuck with it; it broke down on nearly every journey.

The other day my old lorry came back from the depot, repaired and completely serviced. My mate who had crashed it was no longer with it. He's been sent off somewhere else. Of course I asked for my lorry back, and my friend the lieutenant duly obliged, so you see I've got the knack of finding the right path. As far as my lorry is concerned I'm as happy as a sand boy.

Things have changed here: we are no longer engaged in dragging pieces of equipment about, but are once again supplying the front. We are camped about 10 km behind the line. Occasionally a shell lands near us but we can't hear the small arms fire and are less exposed. The stillness doesn't bother me too much. It's a bit boring, but don't criticise me too much, as I've done my bit. Sixteen months of turmoil is enough. Any column-dodger coming here would tremble all over, but for those of us who are used to being at the front it's not too bad. At the moment we aren't having to work too hard, because this area has not been fought over, and the trains are still running quite close to the front. We are here in reserve in case there is an advance.

Also, little Mum, I've rented a little room. It's got a good bed, a table and three chairs. At least I can sleep under cover and when there's nothing to do I can work. Living like an animal for a year is enough. You will be surprised to hear it, but in my spare time I have taken up my natural history again. It used to bore me stiff, but now I find great pleasure in it. I'm getting to the bottom of it and find that I can remember it much better. I'm a year older, and a year of war changes a person a lot. So I'm devouring great chunks of it enthusiastically; I shall write you ever longer and more frequent letters on condition that you do the same for me, which to be fair I have always found that you do. It was a lucky chance that I found the room. Some time ago a shell destroyed half of the house; the owner didn't want to live there anymore, and decided to rent the rooms out. My mate Roussillon has taken one of them and I have got the other, at 15 francs a month. That's money well spent to get us through the hard nights. Will the arrangement last? I don't know, but for the moment I don't care tuppence about the Boches and their shells.

So you can see that you don't have to worry much about me. If I stay here long the second winter ought to be a great deal better than the first.

Apart from that nothing much new. Oh, no, I forgot – there are going to be more periods of leave. I reckon that in three months or so I shall come home to see you and hug you again. There is going to be a regular cycle of leave, which sounds good except when you think that it means they aren't thinking that the war is about to end.

Big hugs,

Pierre

Here's a picture of me on the sand dunes.

Pierre mentions an anticipated move for the first time. Rumour had it his unit was entraining for Champagne, Alsace or Salonika.

Pierre astride a sand dune near Dunkirk. (Private collection)

16 November 1915

To start with, nothing much in the way of news. It seems more likely that we will be sent to Alsace than to Serbia. I hope that that is true, because you would be upset otherwise. Personally I shall be happy to get out of here, as a Taube has just come to drop bombs on us. I had a narrow escape: the shell fragment I enclose embedded itself in the wood of the steering wheel, and there were plenty more in the tyres. I don't know how they missed me! I don't mind telling you I was shaken up. During the evening, to restore my spirits, I drank a bit too much with the lads and was completely zonked. It was quite pardonable, as we have quite a few moments of high emotion like that.

A big hug but a quick one. We leave tonight and the weather is foul.

Pierre

18 November 1915

Dear Little Mum,

Nothing much to tell, except that while we're waiting for our posting they've put us back on blasted night driving, in an area to the right of where we usually go. Good God! What weather! Rain, mud, ice and mud.

I don't regret joining up, but when I think about my schoolmates warming their toes in the back areas it really annoys me. At the same time I envy them: I wouldn't mind a few months smoking my pipe to unfreeze the end of my nose, moaning about the weather, and then in the fine spring weather I'll come running to give you a hug.

Did you get the boots? I put a little note in them. They were fine except that they were both for the same foot! The shop will sort them out, and when he has I'll be glad to have them back. I shall be able to splash about in the mud like a kid!

Can't write more, as I've got to drain the engine so that it won't freeze tonight.

Big kisses,

Pierre

27 November 1915

Dear Mum and Dad,

I've just got in. Many many thanks for the money order and the fine boots. They'll come in handy, as for the last four days we've been floundering about in 25 cm. of snow.

It's pretty dodgy driving the lorries on the frozen snow. Yesterday I was driving along at about ten at night, without lights but thinking that I was following the road, when I plunged the lorry head first into a ditch. It took us half the night to get it out, but we amused ourselves with a snowball fight.

Big kisses,

Pierre

2 December 1915

Dear Mum,

I'm not your son for nothing! You reproach me very kindly for knowing how to make myself agreeable to you and Grandpa. I could say the same about you! You're very clever at finding out my deepest feelings. So the other day you got me to admit something that I'm sure made you happy, and your letter today confirms it.

There are two things I would like to mention. You think I'm faltering, but I have turned things over and over in my mind for many months in these extraordinary conditions of risk, troubles and hard slog, at the front, a place where only one's will enables one to hang on and survive. The will is an essential element for success. The other thing is your saying that you sometimes lose confidence in me. It was wrong of you to say that and it has caused me grief. When I was a kid you trusted me, and now I'm a man you don't? You owe me some big hugs to make up for the hurt you caused me by those few words.

Now, Mother, why are you probing even more deeply into my soul? Why have you sent me the photo of Marie-Antoinette? And now you say you don't know your son's heart, when in reality you know it a hundred times better than I know it myself. I won't hide from you that when I went off to war I was full of thoughts of her, but little by little she went out of my mind, and when I came home on leave I was quite cool about her. And then, wallop! You send me her photo, and now I glance at it in the morning, and at lunchtime, and at night. And I've enjoyed it.

Big hugs for you and Dad,

Pierre

6 December 1915

Dear Mum

I'm very surprised that you haven't had the card in which I told you I had received the two money orders. Don't worry that I'll rush out and spend them – I haven't had the chance. As soon as I get money I put it in my wallet straight away against the

Marie-Antoinette Barthe, "Mimi" (Private collection)

moment when my pay runs out. With this I shan't run the risk of being caught without anything if we are suddenly moved again.

Here's a list of my monthly expenses

- A litre of wine every two days at 20 sous a litre – 15 francs
- Washing and mending – 10 francs
- From time to time it's hard when I come back tired out around 11 p.m., and I've got to go back on guard duty at 2 a.m., and get on the road again in the morning. I sometimes then pay someone else to do my guard duty so that one of the poor souls whose home area has been occupied can earn a few pence – 20 francs
- The biggest item is when we go off on our own. I can't buy just for two, so we have to eat at some restaurant or out of tins, which gets expensive. My new co-driver is a good chap but he is penniless, and you wouldn't want me to eat alone, with him looking on at me, so we share. He pays me back by helping with the maintenance of the vehicle, at which he is skilful – 40 francs

I've counted in that all sorts of odds and ends like soap and laces, so you see that I haven't been splashing out.

From 18th to 31st December, there were eleven short letters and cards. Pierre was fully absorbed with his military duties, so there appears to have been little time to write. He requested money rather than Christmas gifts.

23 December 1915

Happy Christmas Mum and Dad, Dear Popo, Grandpa and Grandma,

What's happened to the Christmas Eves[5] we used to have? I don't fancy trying to re-create the atmosphere on some bit of roadside, but even that might be a bit of fun and I would enjoy thinking of you all.

Big hugs,

Pierre

25 December 1915

Dear Grandpa,

Many thanks for your money order. It arrived in the nick of time, as I hadn't got a penny. We had a pretty miserable Christmas Eve on the move: someone fixed it for us to drive all night!

Got to rush,

Big hugs,

Pierre

---

5   In France, it is customary to celebrate on Christmas Eve and welcome the first moments of Christmas Day; these celebrations also incorporate Midnight Mass attendance. [T's N]

3

I'm really looking forward to going abroad

On 21 February 1916, the German Fifth Army assaulted the fortress town of Verdun, thus commencing a titanic struggle that raged on for six months. Throughout the succeeding March, bitter fighting occurred along the River Meuse at Mort-Homme ('Dead Man') Hill, Côte 304 and Caures Wood. The war, now into its seventeenth month, found Pierre at the eastern extremity of the western front. He wrote home regularly, even if there was little to say.

8 January 1916 (*to his father*)
You have too big a heart to cause grief to your little wife and your children who love you so much. Also, Dad, I hope that if by any chance you were to come up to the front you would have enough will power to keep to your diet. I'm talking to you as an old soldier, because the only things we can do here are drinking and smoking, which would be disastrous for you. Does it irritate you, me giving you advice?

12 January 1916
I've got to go to Bar-le-Duc to collect some new American vehicles, and then I'm going East. Hugs, Pierre

27 January 1916
Nothing much new. We haven't yet got back to Versailles where I'm hoping to get some leave while they load the lorries. I hope it will be soon. Until that happens we are staying here quietly away from the front, with only a few routine jobs to do. If this tranquil existence goes on much longer I shall think I've been ambushed, but with any luck it won't. You know me well enough to know that I couldn't put up with it. I'm really looking forward to setting sail for the East, which should be a fine sight. I'm not expecting to end up out in Salonika with Mr. Cavayé[1], but if it's Egypt with the Sphinx and the Pyramids it will be better in every respect, particularly as to the weather.

At last Pierre arrived at Voisins-le-Bretonneux near Versailles. He was uncertain about obtaining leave before this new chapter in his life, so requested some useful things:

11 February 1916
- Twelve rolls of film for the West Pocket Kodak
- Some good tinned food (apparently it is much sought after out there)
- A Browning revolver with magazine and bullets (ask Grandpa)
- Guide books for Egypt and Serbia
- A first aid kit (ask doctor Alibert)

---

1   A family friend.

13 February 1916

Dear Little Mum,

It's Sunday, so what should I do but write you a long letter, and then everyone will be happy.

The first thing to say is that I'm writing this in the salon of a chateau! It's a fine building on a beautiful estate, though the bedding isn't up to much. It's just a layer of straw in the empty room where we've fetched up this afternoon, and it's none too warm either. It would be great for a peace-time summer holiday, but at the moment it looks like a barracks with our guns, helmets and haversacks hanging up everywhere, and it stinks of soldiers and pipe smoke. It's in this delightful place that I am stretched out on the straw having a little chat with you.

This morning, not having much to do, I went to mass – it's been a long time since I did that.

Mum, you're going to complain that I'm always asking for money: please remember that now we are out of the battle zone we are on half rations with no wine and no tobacco. For a man of 19 this is hard to take! Luckily I've got a few pence left, and every day after we've eaten the tiny portion they give us, we have to buy more to bulk it out. Every day we have to buy a liter of wine and something to smoke. Some days we don't get anything at all and have to find a restaurant. Thank goodness when we get on board ship all that will sort itself out *(he asks for 200 francs to meet his expenses before the voyage and lists the things he has to pay for)*. Did you know that Mr. Barthe is still at Bretigny? It is only 20 kms away so one of these days I am going to borrow a bike and go and see him. I am sure he will give me good advice as usual.

Mr. Barthe was not alone in Bretigny: he has brought his family, among them Marie-Antoinette.

14 February 1916

I have had a letter from the Barthes at Bretigny. Mrs Barthe has written to me saying how much they will enjoy seeing me and hugging me. Result – one of these days I will borrow our unit's motorbike and pop over to see them. Oh Mum, I shall be very happy to see Marie-Antoinette before I go. It will be very nice for me because I have taken a fancy to that young lady.

Little Mum please excuse me for telling my secrets – I talk to you like a big sister. Keep the secret or look out!

Finally obtaining the desired three-day leave, Pierre managed to spend a day and a half at home at the end of February. At the beginning of March there are a few short letters, and then:

7 March 1916

Dear Mum

At last I have got your letter that you wrote since my return here. It seemed a long time before I had it and I have read and re-read it several times, remembering the days I spent at home. I was struck by the passage where you spoke about our goodbye. You said that you cried after the door had shut behind me. You tell me it was a very motherly thing to do and I thought it didn't disturb you.

Pierre on home leave February 1916. (Private collection)

It was such a natural thing that it shouldn't have upset me and yet I felt a tug at my heart when I read it. Thank you for it. It tells me how much you love us, your children, little Popo and your big soldier. It touched me that you were able to admit it in spite of the fact that it might upset me. Mum you are brave and so I have to be brave and although I am far away I give you a big hug to show how happy your big son is to have a little Mum like you.

You ask me why I walked all the way from Versailles to Voisins. First of all there were about 20cms of snow on the ground and the taxis were asking ridiculous prices so I just wandered along to the restaurant and had a nice dinner with the taxi fare. I don't need to go on about it because you know how happy a soldier is with his belly full and his pipe in his mouth. So you see everything turned out for the best. For the summer clothes don't bother about sending them. I have not yet got the lamp and batteries but I am expecting them soon. As for the quinine tablets I promise you I will take them before I set sail. Let me know how many to take and how to take them.

Bad news about Georges Forestié, but a soldier must be philosophical as far as he can, and life is not a big deal. I think I have mentioned all the things you asked about, so here is my news. At the moment it is 11 o'clock at night and I am sitting in a soft armchair with my feet on a hot stove and (look out, Grandpa!) with my pipe in my mouth. I am in a nice little room where everything is completely peaceful. What I am actually doing is deputising for the lieutenant in his office overnight to pick up any orders that arrive. I have to stay awake all night, keep an eye on the paperwork in the office and sweep up and light the fire before the lieutenant arrives in the morning. Because everybody else is asleep I draw up the armchair near the fire, fill my pipe from the tobacco jar on the table (it is good stuff) and since I am not very good at lighting the stove, I just cram it full so that it will still be alight in the morning. I'm not paying for it!

This night duty is something we all do in turn, and like every pleasant duty I only get to do it once a month. It is a pity because I could well sign up to keep warm like this every night. And what can I find to do better in this peace, Mum, than to spend time chatting with you? And it is a fact that when I write to you I feel as if I have been magicked [sic] among you. It seems that I am really speaking to you and that you can hear every word that I say. And I am sure that when you are at table and reading my letters you too will have the feeling that it is really little Pierre himself, there, who is telling you his little tales. Through letters one can live as intensely as if we were together and in some ways it is even more charming to be far away. Everything one says becomes a little more entertaining and a little more forceful and when you finish your letters by saying "your Mum gives you a big hug with all her heart" you can be sure that I am as happy as if you were hugging me. The only bother is that to hug you back I have only got your photo and it is only paper ...

As to our departure it is now quite certain, but we don't know when. I am here waiting for the call. I expect to hear within a week. And then, Whammo! I can't wait to sail away. I'm bored stiff doing nothing here. You would perhaps hope that we are not sailing, and then, off to Verdun. As they say here "it's out of question": go back to the Western Front? Enough with that! But now that we've got the idea that we are going far away, it would be a big disappointment. They wanted us to go and we are going willingly. Don't bother us with that any longer.

I am still hoping to go and see the Barthes. Our officer is a good fellow so when he gets here tomorrow everything will be in good order and I shall be able to ask him for a bit of time off. As soon as I have got the pass in my pocket I shall be away. Perhaps (and I can't promise) I shall be able to get over from Marseilles to give you a hug. Apparently they give you 4 days' embarkation leave and if that is the case that will be fine. Let us assume that it is impossible, and then we will be all the happier if it does take place. You can see, Mum, that today nobody needed to twist my arm to make me write to you. Every day a line or two, yes and when I am not bone idle, a longer letter. This evening I am so comfy that I could go on forever, but I will finally come to an end little Mum with a big hug for you, Popo, Granny and Grandpa.

Your young Serbian, Pierre

11 March 1916

Dear little Mum,

Yesterday I wrote to little Popo because she had sent me two lovely letters. I had better write one to you quickly so that you are not jealous of my sister.

Anyway I have some good things to tell you: the day I spent with the Barthes was very nice. I managed to get a leave the day before yesterday, much to my delight. It didn't seem long to go the 8kms to Versailles. To get a good connection I went through Paris and at 11 o'clock I got to Bretigny. It took a bit of time but eventually I found the Chateau Lafontaine. I cannot tell you how full my heart was in seeing the pleasure they had in seeing me. Everybody was delighted to see me and during dinner it was a bit like being at home again. We had a good chat and I really enjoyed the relaxed atmosphere that you only get among good friends. They made me so happy during the day that it will be a memory which will be a great comfort to me on days when I am feeling down.

The ladies of the family are still very good fun. Magui (*Marie-Antoinette's younger sister*) is very pretty and Marie-Antoinette ... I can't quite tell you exactly without using language that might upset you! Barthe is still the same as ever. I went round Étampes with him, which was so interesting that we missed the train on the way back. Another lovely meal where they spoiled me as you can well imagine and at 8 o'clock we set off for the station.

There we were, the soldier in the middle, Mr. Barthe on one arm and Marie-Antoinette on the other in the bright moonlight, these were lovely moments. It was so lovely that when we got to the station the Paris train had gone. It didn't matter because Mr. Barthe helped me to alter the details on my pass, and I got back to Voisins at 3 o'clock in the morning.

Nothing has changed in our situation, still waiting and waiting, which is beginning to be a pain but we must be patient, eh, Mum? So I finish by giving you a big hug and another for everybody there.

Pierre

P.S. Thank you for the paté and rolls of film. Did you send me the torch and batteries? I haven't had them yet.

12 March 1916

Dear little Mum,

At last I got the post. Your letters of 2nd and 6th arrived together yesterday. One of them made me laugh when you were talking about getting an inner tube. You referred to another letter which I have not yet had, nor the torch and batteries. Perhaps the parcels have got lost and will arrive in a few days. No point in moaning about it.

You were saying that you were advising me to find an inner tube. Are you kidding? To blow it up and put it on would take so much effort that I had better get a lifeboat. Let us be serious. Don't waste time looking for one, this is what I suggest: in a port like Marseilles I am sure they sell the little cork life-belts which are quite adequate to support you in the water and not get in the way and I promise I will buy one, although I am sure they will be completely useless. I have got the feeling that the voyage is going to be fun and our time spent over there interesting and entertaining, as Marie-Antoinette whispered in my ear the other day.

Oh Mum don't get upset that I am whispering in young ladies ears! I can see a smile on your face and I allow myself to tell you a little secret – you know you want me to (keep the secret or else). This time we left each other better friends than we had been at the time of my last leave. This time I was really smitten by her and I must be getting more serious because I liked her more and more. I must tell you that I think she was very impressed to see me all dressed up as a soldier with my cap over my ear ... .

When I got there, something very nice happened. I am only saying this to you because it was really funny. I was just arriving at the drive of the Chateau, a couple of steps behind an officer and there, coming towards us, was a charming figure which I immediately recognised. When she got level with the officer, he greeted her very

Tree-lined avenue leading to Chateau Lafontaine Bretigny. (Private collection)

politely as if he wanted to have a chat.

He had not noticed me behind him and he was astonished to see the squaddie and the young lady falling into each other's arms and hugging each other like two kids. You should have seen the old officer, it was so comical that we both burst out laughing and he, being a nice chap, laughed along with us to see us so happy. He was a friend of Mr. Barthe.

A nice little tale, eh, Mum?

I am thinking that you enjoy hearing the little secrets of your grown up boy. I am speaking to you more as to my big sister than as to my Mum!

There you are, you thought I had nothing to say but whenever I have got anything to tell you, only idleness or depression can stop me saying it.

Big hugs to everyone,

Pierre

Monday 13 March 1916

Dear little Mum

It is a lovely spring morning and it has put an end to the lousy weather which we have been having. It is really wonderful to feel the warm sunshine dispelling the continual damp in which we have been living. It makes us feel alive again and fills us with enthusiasm and courage. Time to write to Mum to give her a taste of this little moment of happiness.

We are really getting to be like kids again with our moods dependent on a little bit of sunshine and warm weather. Our spirits lift a bit and we feel good again. When the weather is grey and miserable it is hardly surprising you feel yourself overtaken by melancholy and negative thoughts; that is when the black mood gets on you and you look back sadly at old times, the house and the family, and you would give anything to be there again.

But Mum, that is not the case at all today. I am leaning against the trunk of a tree, the sun in my eyes and what am I dreaming about? I am dreaming about my own homeland, the only one which has sunshine like here. One feels one's French heart beating again and one only has one desire, to go home; but it is not just that, because we must win the victory first, so that we can live there peacefully and free.

Mum, the sun is making my head spin, and I've lost track of what I am talking about. The main thing is to keep up communication with you and thus to live a few minutes together.

Yesterday I had a little note from Dad, which I enjoyed reading particularly because I sense that things are getting better there. Also I have written him a letter, which I am sure he will enjoy, in which I have, very tactfully, given him some good advice.

Nothing more new. When are we going? Not long now for sure, but they are boring us stiff.

Big hugs to you Mum and everyone there.

Pierre

4

Goodbye, France

The Macedonian campaign intrigued me. I felt the need to gather more information when contextualizing Pierre's self-censored correspondence. The grand strategic situation prior to the campaign was extremely complicated. At the conclusion of the Second Balkan War (1912-13) Serbia was supported by the Triple Entente (France, Britain and Russia) whilst Bulgaria and the Ottoman Empire were aligned with the rival Triple Alliance (Germany, Austria, Hungary and Italy – the latter joining the Entente in spring 1915). Following the recognised failure of the Gallipoli campaign, French and British troops disembarked at the neutral Greek port of Salonika to support hard-pressed Serbia. With Belgrade in enemy hands and the remainder of the country overrun by German, Austrian, Bulgarian and Ottoman invaders, the new Allied front lapsed into stalemate. The first major Allied offensive followed in autumn 1916. On 17 November, the Greek frontier town of Monastir (now known as Bitola) was captured and it is almost certain that Pierre Suberviolle was there at the time. Perusing his letters, photographs and annotated map, it is possible to retrace his footsteps.

In May 1916 we find him in the Strouma valley east of Salonika where the fort of Rupel had been abandoned to the Bulgars. From here he went to Serres to the north-east of Salonika passing through Lahana on the way (he took a photograph of a peasant girl near a fountain there). In July 1916 he describes himself as driving round the arid mountains, and in October 1916 he finally sees action against the Bulgars "amidst dry mountains and superb lakes". He camped at Sorovich (the present day Amynteo) west of Salonika, where he took several pictures of Bulgarian prisoners. In December 1916, he was near Monastir (today Bitola), billeted in Vakuskoy where he was under the Bulgarian shells. In January and February 1917 he was in the mountains again with "lots of snow and bitter cold". In March 1917 he was still in Albania and he spent the spring working in a liaison capacity driving a car. With just a single companion he drove as far as Lake Presba, but as might be expected, he says nothing about what they were doing there. In August and September 1917 he was officially appointed "Driver to the commanding officer of the Transport Services of the French Eastern Army" and in this capacity he drove right across Greece as far as the Gulf of Corinth, buying postcards in Delphi and Athens.

We pick up the story at the moment that Pierre had been awaiting for such a long time, the embarkation at Marseilles. He writes on the back of a postcard with a picture of the L'Arc de Triomphe on it marked "begun in 1806 by Napoleon I to the glory of the French Armies, the monument was finally completed under King Louis Phillipe at a cost of 9 million francs. It suffered badly during the commune uprising in 1871, when it was hit by more than 2,000 shells".

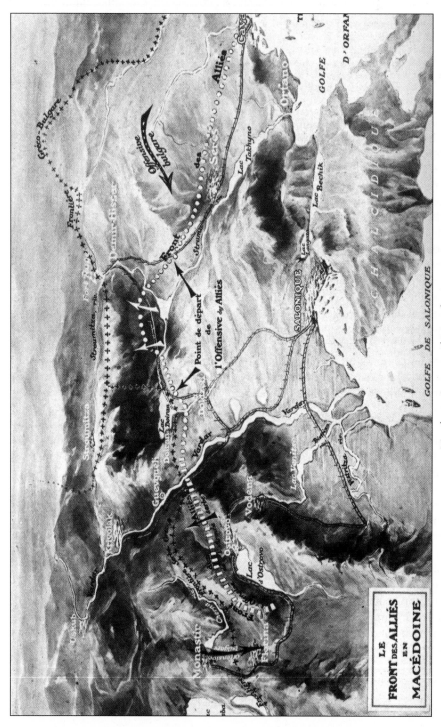

Northern Greece and Macedonia

Lorries were packed into large wooden crates prior to embarkation.
Photo by Pierre Suberviolle. (Private collection)

Paris, 14 March 1916

At last we're going away. We have driven the lorries to be boxed up, and tomorrow, on to Marseilles.

Hugs,
Pierre

23 March 1916

Dear Dad

Everything is fine, superb and magnificent. We have fine weather, and the sea is very rough, which I find great fun (because I have not been seasick yet). They have put us in the second hold of the ship, the stench is terrible (tar, vomit and seawater), but I can hack it and even find it quite funny: I am nearly always on the deck anyway. Hoping that everything continues to go well.

Big hugs,
Pierre

From Salonika: Telegram received at Montauban, 26 March 1916:

Good crossing – good health – keep on sending the money – Kisses – Pierre

Salonika, 25 March 1916

Dear Dad

I am sending you a quick word because a boat is about to leave for France. I have written a long letter to Mum and you can get from her all the gossip about the voyage.

The main thing is we had a fantastic crossing, with just 2 scary moments: a submarine followed us for 70 kms as we were approaching Malta, but thanks to the speed of our boat we got away. Then when we were off Cape Matapan (where the

Sailing to Salonika. Photo by Pierre Suberviolle. (Private collection)

"Provence" sank)[1], we had some nervous moments, but we were escorted by a torpedo boat and got through safely. Here I am living in a big tented camp[2] (like the Buffalo Circus). It is scorching hot but it is a good life. I reckon we will be fine here, much better than in France. We are only a short way out of Salonika so we can get anything we need.

Thanks for the 50 francs. I used it to buy food for the voyage.

Big hugs,

Pierre

Salonika, 26 March 1916

Dear Mum

Safely in port, in good health, so here are my first impressions. Safely in port yes, but not without some emotion, the kind of emotion that makes you feel really alive and in fact I was very deeply moved by what I have gone through.

You remember that we were suddenly ordered from Voisins-le-Bretonneux on 15th March, I think I mentioned to you how wonderful I thought the trip to Marseilles was. Oh France you are the most beautiful of countries, and it is from far away that one can appreciate you best! We stayed just 3 days at Marseilles and on the 20th, without having been able to enjoy the beautiful Canebière[3], we were on the way to Toulon. We got there at midday, marched through the town with our rifles on our shoulders and straight away got onto the ship. I have got so many things to say and I will have to explain them all one by one when you ask me about them. I promise faithfully to write to you every day as much as possible.

I was saying that we got on the boat about 1 o'clock in the afternoon. It was a fine ship called the Theodore Mante, where they put us in the second hold towards the front of the ship. An unforgettable sight it is true but very hot and very smelly. Every

---

1   The troop transport *Provence II* was sunk on March 1st; 870 out of 1700 passengers were rescued.
2   Pierre was probably billeted at Zeitnilick (other spelling Zeitenlick), an enormous tented facility.
3   La Canebière, the most famous avenue in Marseilles, is what the Champs-Elysées is to Paris. [T's N]

Steamship *Theodore Mante*. (Private collection)

possible minute I could I was up on the deck. At 5 o'clock p.m. we set sail and it was goodbye, France. We waved goodbye with some feeling and off we went on to the blue waves, to be thrown about by the pitching and rolling! I enjoyed all the confusion and so far have not been seasick for a minute, though a number of my companions have been giving the fish something to eat!

On the 22nd in the afternoon at about 3 o'clock we saw a submarine behind us and for a few minutes we were really scared. Our boat forged through the waves and thank goodness it was quick because without that we would have had it! The submarine followed us for about 70kms. We passed an English ship going the other way and about half an hour later we heard a huge explosion, so we think it must have been sunk.

Happily we weren't far from Malta and at 5 o'clock we entered the port at full speed. We were safe. We stopped there for 2 hours and picked up the survivors from the "Provence". Then we set off again, this time escorted by a torpedo boat.

It soon proved its worth because as we were rounding Cape Matapan there was another submarine alarm. It must have feared the torpedo boat because it dived and made off. The rest of the voyage went peacefully and we were able to enjoy the view of the beautiful coast of Greece, the Cyclades, the Sporades and all across the Aegean Sea.

And so we arrived without any hitches at Salonika yesterday, 25th March, which was the Sabbath. We arrived at 10 o'clock in the morning having crossed from France in record time, just 4 days and 5 nights. Before this, even the fastest boats took 8 days. Amazing what you can do with a rocket up your a**e.

And now here we are in a magnificent tented camp which reminds me of the Buffalo Circus. It is scorching hot and the country is very beautiful and an interesting study in people's customs. We have struck gold coming here. I think we are going to stay in Salonika itself to provide transport for the port. The result of that will be that we shall be quite safe and will have everything we want and we shall not be unhappy. I don't need you to send me much apart from a little bit of French tobacco. The only downside is that everything is very expensive so please keep sending me money on a regular basis. Living here is expanding my horizons and my education and I am glad that the war has given me the chance of seeing this place.

— Habitants de Salonique et réfugiés serbes au camp franco-anglais de Zeinitlik —

Zeitnitlik Camp, Salonika. (*Le Miroir,* 19 December 1915)

Did you get my telegram – it was 18 sous a word but I thought it was worth it to save you from worry. Got to go now Mum, because the post is being collected.

Great big hugs from your little boy Pierre

The ancient town of Salonika was first settled by the Greeks in 315 BC. A cosmopolitan city that attracted a myriad of different races and creeds, it was a major port of call for ships travelling to Asia and Africa via the Suez Canal. Under Greek rule since1912, it had approximately150,000 inhabitants including Slavs, Romanians and Jews. Simultaneously appalling and magnificent, it had a picturesque, albeit seedy, old quarter and modern port facilities, which the Allies duly enlarged to cope with increased military demands.

Salonika, 29 March 1916

Dear Popo,

It is 1 o'clock in the afternoon, it is bloody hot and we are on duty. Only big Peterkin is relaxing and rather than levelling the ground for a vehicle park I've slipped away behind the tents and found a shady place to write to my big kid sister.

I have got some interesting news to tell you. Life is pretty odd here. We are camped on the edge of Salonika in the Jewish quarter, where the men wear skirts and the women wear trousers – just like your Algerian doll. It is very oriental: the roads, if you can call them that, are footpaths with big ditches in them caused by the water coming off the mountains, the houses have flat roofs and they are very densely packed.

Salonika. Photo by Pierre Suberviolle. (Private collection)

The little windows are curtained but you can sometimes see a person within wearing a pink or blue veil. All very fascinating.

I would tell you a lot of other things, but we are very busy. Our lorries have not come yet, which means we get all the hard labouring jobs to do. When they arrive it will be more comfortable.

I wrote yesterday to Mr. Cavayé – I hope to see him one of these days, if he can get here. If not, I will try and sort out a way of getting to see him on one of the army lorries. Big hugs to little Mimi and everyone there, Pierre

P.S. At the moment I don't need anything, but if you could find any nice pâté and a bit of tobacco I should be happy to have that.

6 April 1916 (*he describes his meeting with Mr. Cavayé and goes on ...*)
Apart from that, little Mum, as far as the climate is concerned it is lovely. We have just been vaccinated against cholera so we are now proof against that and typhoid. We still have to take a quinine tablet every morning, but that doesn't bother me at all. Nothing for you to worry your head about. Now about my hair. My lovely hair, which I was so proud of! I summoned up my courage to have it cut short, and how! My head looks a real sight. I chose to do it because of the heat. I am sending you a little lock of it: keep it, because I shall enjoy seeing it again.

I wait like Sister Anne and when the postman comes he has never got anything for me. I heave a big sigh and in the depths of my despair I light my pipe in the hope that when I come back tomorrow full of hope there will be something there for me. How happy I shall be.

For the moment, Mum, I don't need anything much except possibly for one of your nice patés. Oh there is one thing, I have broken the stem of my pipe (a very serious matter) so when you next go to Toulouse could you find the pipe seller next to the Café de la Paix in the Place du Capitole and ask him if he has got another one like the one I have drawn at the bottom of the letter, made of ebonite? If he has not got one he can surely get one.

A band of Romanian brigands. (Private collection)

We have M. Cavaye's account, sent to Pierre's mother, Augusta, of his meeting with Pierre. This is written on the back of a postcard depicting Romanian brigands.

6 April 1916
Dear Madam,

I saw Pierre yesterday evening and I hasten to tell you that he made an excellent impression on me. I had had the pleasure of a letter from him after his arrival and I took the opportunity on this my first trip to Salonika to go and see him. It wasn't very convenient because I had the misfortune to turn up just at the moment he was leaving camp to go and get the stocks of petrol in his lorry. I waited till he came back and I was just on the point of giving up when I had the good fortune to meet him at the corner of the street. He was very pleasantly surprised because he wasn't expecting to see me at such a time and place. I went with him to the end of the road but it was very late and he had to go sooner than I would have wished. The main thing for you is that I found him in excellent health, he looked well and was enjoying the experience of seeing a new country. His camp is outside the town in the Jewish quarter. He won't get bored there because he will have the chance of seeing the Orient in detail and I hope he has got the sense to do it wisely and moderately.

Salonika, 12 April 1916
Dear Mum

I haven't written for two days but it isn't my fault. On Monday morning we set off on a long journey across Greece and we only came back yesterday night.

Oh Mum, what a fantastic journey it was! Exhausting, certainly, but it was so beautiful and completely different. These were not ordinary journeys. Imagine the

Gavarnie road in the Pyrenees, but steeper and indeed hardly marked out. You have got rocks, holes and weeds all tangled together and everywhere tortoises lined up as if for a battle who retract their heads into their shells when they see us passing. Then you have got parrots, swans and birds of prey wheeling round on every side, astonished but not at all frightened by the noise of the engines. You have got to think I am spinning you a yarn but it is just what I saw.

Think as well that this is around 2500 feet up which we've travelled from sea level and taking only twelve miles to get here. There are steep climbs and the lorries have a devil of a job to get up them; you have to keep your wits about you because the track is just about as wide as the lorries with the mountain on one side and a 600 foot drop on the other. There are bends so sharp that you have to do 3 point turns. It is a real death trap but charming nevertheless.

At every turn another magnificent horizon opens up, beautiful by the vastness and by the special something which you find in this region. It is like the Pyrenees but completely empty and arid without a living soul 60 miles in any direction. The only village we came across was completely ruined having been destroyed in the Greco/Turkish war in 1913, and the whole area has often been fought over since the war began.

And so 60 miles out and 60 miles back, this was our journey and I have come back full of wonder. In my next letter I'll tell you about the town we went to.

Now let's talk business. Thank you for your letter of the 27th, the first I have had and thanks for the 20 francs. Between Grandpa and you I would like to have that much every week. 80 francs a month isn't that much, especially when you consider that contrary to what the gossips say, we always loose 13½ % on the exchange rate.

I wrote asking you for some good driving glasses and some sunglasses. I would like two boxes of 25 cartridges for the 7.65 revolver and a new leather holster, because the one I have got is ruined. I would also like you to send my little compass.

Big hugs,
Pierre

Salonika, 28 April 1916

Dear little Dad,

I really enjoyed your long letter. It is a long time since you have written such a long one. I hope you are being sensible and following your diet: you know how happy it makes us all when you do. I give you big hugs. It is not a joke what I am telling you, it is a considered judgement based on what you said in your letter.

For the moment I have got lots of things to say: as far as the service is concerned we are occupied the whole time with refuelling and resupplying. In the fine weather it is lovely. You cross fields and streams, because there are hardly any roads, but when it is raining it is a nightmare and you neither move backwards or forwards. What I find fascinating is the novelty of everything we see – a twisting road with its surface cut into by streams running down it, winds up the side of the mountain. To left and right we see houses painted pink or violet, so close that you can nearly touch them and in the distance a minaret, surrounded by cypress trees, lifts its slender and gracious tower into the sky.

And over everything the golden sun makes the earth seem redder, the houses more violet, the minaret whiter and the cypress trees darker. And to complete the picture a

Sérès. Photo by Pierre Suberviolle. (Private collection)

few veiled heads from which only the jays' eyes look out make their appearance at the sash-windows.

That is briefly what we see in the Jewish or Turkish quarters of Salonika, which are the only interesting parts of it. The middle of the town is completely cosmopolitan and characterless.

In my next letter I will describe some other places to you, but for the moment I am in good health and the heat isn't bothering us too much. As far as my helmet is concerned, I haven't got one yet, and if the army doesn't give us any you can buy them for 3 francs each.

Dear Dad, I finish my letter with big hugs.

Pierre

P.S. ... and if you want to please me write me more long letters.

Some of Pierre's photographs demonstrate a keen personal interest in this exotic land. We find pictures of a Turkish farm and windmill; Macedonian peasants and a young woman near a fountain, as well as children. These photos were probably taken shortly after his arrival. It can only be surmised that he didn't have the time or perhaps the desire to obtain additional souvenirs, but they are valuable records of a period now long vanished. Sometime later it appears that he was quite happy to purchase picture postcards of Salonika, Delphi and Athens.

Salonika, 10 May 1916
Dear Mum and Dad,

At last I have got time to write you a letter, which will soon be on its way. We have just spent a fortnight in the middle of nowhere in the heart of Macedonia. It's forbidden to tell you where exactly we were but I am just going to give you a glimpse of what life is like. In the area where we are working there are just a few tiny villages in the whole area about 120 miles across. All the rest are mountains over 2,000 feet, completely bare and arid. During the day you are roasting at 50 degrees in the shade

Turkish windmill. Photo by Pierre Suberviolle. (Private collection)

Turkish farmstead. Photo by Pierre Suberviolle. (Private collection)

and in the night we freeze and are often completely enveloped in the clouds. We get fed but it is a bit monotonous and as to wine, forget it – you drink from the brooks. We don't suffer too much from this because like camels we are now able to march for several days without eating properly.

For all that the climate and the food haven't made a jot of difference to my good health. My skin is now a fine brown colour worthy of the finest Turk.

All these little details are fascinating, and at every turn we are continually surprised at what we see, whether it is on a long drive or in coming out of the tent in the morning.

Here is a brief summary of one of my days. We get up about 4 o'clock in the morning and go up to the top of the mountain to see the sunrise: breathtaking. The best way I can explain it to you is by comparing it to Cauterets or the Gavarnie road. We drink some coffee and then at 6 o'clock we set off and drive the whole day without

Macedonian peasants. Photo by Pierre Suberviolle (Private collection)

stopping. Sixty miles a day on roads like this is pretty dreadful, so when we get back in the evening at 7 o'clock we do a quick a grease of the vehicles and then go to sleep, because by then we are completely exhausted. It is life in the middle of nowhere with news only once a week. Nowhere to buy anything and what there is terribly expensive and nothing whatever to entertain us. The only pleasure we have is lying on a rock, looking at the beautiful eastern sky, smoking a good pipe of tobacco and buying some scarce food.

Oh Mum, in one of your letters, you made me laugh. You made a few suggestions thinking that I was spending my money on carousing! But where and with whom could I do such a thing? The only women we see are Turks or Gypsies plodding along the roads, but they are too dirty and too ugly for us to give them a second glance.

At Salonika one can indeed find things to amuse oneself, but they cost money and believe me you can't get up to much mischief with 17 francs 20 (what I get in Greek money from 20F). The person who told you that Salonika is a town of sin ought to have added that it is so only for the officers and not for us squaddies. You need have no worries on that point.

And so there is absolutely no cause for you to worry. I am sometimes a bit down but you would never be able to guess why. The work we do is very tiring, a hundred times worse than in France, but one thing is missing: the constant roar of the guns and the exploding shells that took our minds off things. It is not the heat of battle here but

Fountain at Lahana. Photo by Pierre Suberviolle. (Private collection)

it is a place where you have always got to go armed and keep a look out wherever you go.

Now Mum, let me thank you for the 20 francs and the 2 parcels which I have received. What a delight to find Easter eggs, chocolate and pâté. I was jumping around like a big kid. The glasses and the sunglasses are excellent and will be absolutely of the greatest value to me. At the moment I don't need anything except to see lots of letters coming on a regular basis and with a little bit of money in each one, which is always welcome. At least I think today you won't have any reason to complain that I have not written enough. I give you great big hugs and please, <u>write often</u>.

Pierre

Salonika, 15 May 1916

Mademoiselle my little sister,

I picked these two little flowers for you on the banks of the River Strouma in the middle of Macedonia. Drops of dew were shining on the petals and weighed down by this light burden they graciously lowered their heads and I picked them still full of the wild smell which reigns in these uninhabited areas.

I hope that in sending you these flowers, Mimi, I am giving you some idea of what it is like here in the bare and arid mountains crowned with clouds, which every morning hide the sun, and the green and swift flowing waters of this river where tortoises swim by the hundred. Perhaps you can imagine an elegant stork standing stock still at the side of the marsh. Standing on one foot with its beak tucked in it waits, and when a frog, unaware of the danger, comes along to enjoy a bit of sunshine, the neck uncoils. There is just a little croak and silence and the bird resumes its posture like a reed.

This, Mimi, is what these flowers are saying to you. Keep them carefully and from time to time when you open the book you will find them again, and straight away you can dream again of these far off countries and you will remember your big brother, who embraces you with all his heart.

Pierre

Turkish children. Photos by Pierre Suberviolle. (Private collection)

His letters in June and July are less frequent and contain less information. This is no doubt because he was working flat out in the terrible heat. He complains of not getting enough letters from home, needs more money and gives advice where it's asked of him.

29 May 1916

You asked me advice about the car. The Rolland Pilain is junk. Don't buy it on any account, you would be better off with a Delage. If it were me, I wouldn't have either of them. I would get the little 10hp Panhard. It may be a little more expensive but it is much better built than the other two. I have watched them over a long time in the service here and it is one of the best little cars there is. That is what I advise but talk to other people and see what they say.

In mid-June, Pierre received disturbing news from his mother. It was during the course of Army veterinary work that his father was injured by a rearing horse and had to undergo surgery. Obviously upset, Pierre doesn't forget the inner man!

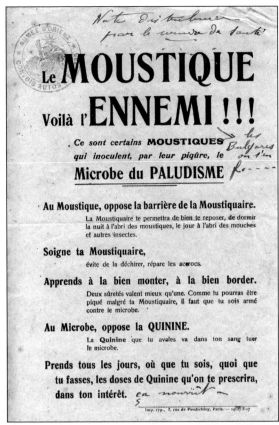

Malaria fact sheet distributed by the French army medical service. Pierre has annotated it with a few mischievous remarks. For example, where it states the "THE MOSQUITO IS YOUR ENEMY", he has written: "the Bulgars, We don't give a toss about them!" At the bottom, doctors advise that troops should take their daily dose of quinine, to which Pierre responds: "It's part of our rations."

19 June 1916

Could you do me a favour and send me every now and then a parcel of tinned food, such things as herring, pâté, tripe, cassoulet, whatever you like. I would be grateful for them. Remember that all we have to eat is meat and rice cooked in fat or water or meat with Italian pasta cooked in fat. No potatoes and no beans, so it is not very appetising. Some nice tinned stuff, particularly homemade, will be very welcome.

24 July 1916 (*to his sister*)

... I will tell you a bit about how I am getting on. If my letters came to an abrupt end it was because I was driving for a whole month on bare and dry tracks through the mountains, completely lost and without any means of communication, but it still annoyed me that I couldn't write to you. It upsets me to think that you worried and I have to hope that at least when you and Mum get a letter after a long gap, it will be correspondingly more welcome. As to your letter, little Popo, you seem to think that I

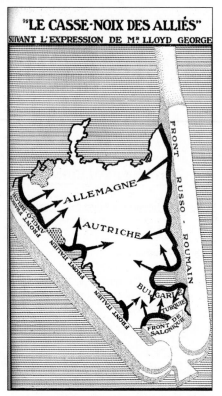

From a British journal article reassuring the general public of a coherent
Allied war strategy. (*Lectures pour tous*, 15 October 1916)

am really ill when you speak of hospitals and nurses. Yes, I was very tired for a while, but
with some willpower, I was able to go on working without a break. How indeed could
I stop when every day we lose lots of men through fever and dysentery? We survivors
have to work all the harder. It was just that I was a bit worn down with so much work
but I haven't got a fever or anything like that. It is all behind me now and I'm fresh and
pink again ... ah no! not pink but fresh and black like a little negro at the breast.

1 August 1916

I think we are advancing rapidly and sometime soon I think you are going to hear
about the Eastern army. The Serbs are already at the front and the Russians started
disembarking yesterday. I don't think they will have to wait long. We are surrounded
by a mixture of flags and uniforms – English, French, Serbs, Russians, Greeks, Hindus,
Annamite *(Annam was part of French Indochina)*, it is worse than the Tower of Babel[4].

---

4   There were, following neutral Greece's declaration of war on the Central Powers in June 1917, 210,000
     French, 138,000 British, 120,000 Serbs, 40,000 Italians and 157,000 Greeks deployed in the Macedonian
     theatre by autumn 1917.

Note: The troops' health in Salonika

Consigned to a campaign viewed, more often than not, by strategists in Paris and London as a sideshow, the most serious enemy faced by the polyglot Salonika Army was disease. Nearly 95 percent of those who served on the Macedonian front during 1915-18 fell ill at one time or another (approximately 360,000 recorded). The most frequent maladies were malaria, dysentery, scurvy and venereal diseases, the sufferers often treated by poorly equipped and overwhelmed medical services. Indeed, malaria reached epidemic proportions. The general state of the area, ravaged by years of conflict, lent itself to outbreaks. Exceptional measures were subsequently taken to improve/reinforce medical facilities and drain marshy areas. These efforts eventually succeeded in almost eliminating malarial outbreaks. (See www. chemins de mémoire.)

5

Lost in the deep blue night

There is a sad irony in the following letter: Pierre is apparently unaware that his father has died on 4 August as a result of an operation he has undergone, his mother having not telegrammed the news. The card dated 29 August from Mr. Naudinet, a friend of the family, which follows this letter, speaks of the effect the news eventually had on Pierre.

21 August 1916

Dear Little Mum,

What must you be thinking of your big son? I've been trying to write to you for four or five days but haven't been able to find a spare minute. They seem to be trying to kill us! I'll just quote you from the *Illustration*: *The soldiers from the eastern army have cheerfully accepted a life comparable with that of people condemned to forced labour.* They are not lying! Fortunately our French good humour enables us to survive and live in hope of better things.

It's no big deal after two years of war; we are so completely committed to a life of sacrifice that nothing that is thrown at us seems out of the ordinary any more. Everything that happens is just 'the war' and our destiny which decrees it. It's only the troubles of our loved ones which get us down: it's now the 21st, and you can imagine how concerned I am at not hearing anything from you since Popo's letter telling me of Dad's operation planned for 2 August.

I am concerned that so much is happening while I am so far away, and unable to share the burden with you or give you courage. Believe me, I am always with you in spirit, and in my thoughts. I do hope that I shall soon get news which will put my fears at rest.

It's quite a while since you wrote, Mum, and yet you must know how much your letters affect me, and how many times I re-read them. Popo is the kindest. Her letters are delightful, and I often have a tear in my eye as I read the tales which she expresses so well in her simple plain words.

What shall I say about myself? Not much. Still in good health; work is normal, and so is the terrible weather. I recently had the pleasure of chatting to Mr. Cavayé again. He is always charming to talk to.

Yesterday I had a wonderful parcel of tinned food from Uncle Eloi, and I'm going to write him a nice letter back about it.

By the time you get this, and I get your reply, winter will be on us. I'm sending you back the summer things I don't need. I'd be grateful if you'd send me two shirts and two flannel long johns, khaki if possible, and a Rasurel jumper.

Big hugs to you and everyone there.

Pierre

A poignant postcard, sent by Mr. Naudinet, a military veterinarian attached to the Serbian army, from Salonica dated 29 August 1916 informed Pierre's grandfather Viguier of a recent encounter with his forlorn grandson.

Dear Mr. Viguier,

I had the pleasure of meeting young Pierre last Saturday (26th), the day after I arrived. The poor chap had not yet received your letter informing him of his father's death, and had received the news in a letter of condolence sent by someone in the family. I found him devastated by the news, but I am sure that the conversation I had with him made him feel a bit better. I told him that you were bearing up splendidly under the terrible blow, which encouraged him. He is made of strong stuff, and the hot and unhealthy climate of Macedonia has not affected him. You won't need telling how happy I was to meet this charming young man for whom I feel affection as if he were my own younger brother. I would have liked to keep in regular touch with him, but unfortunately my duty takes me far from Salonica (I'm off to Florina); I hope, however, that I may be able to shake his hand at least once a month.

Please pass on my respects to Mrs Viguier and Mrs Suberviolle, and give Paulette a big kiss on each cheek. Tell her that I have carried out her instruction to do the same to Pierre. As for you, dear Viguier, a good strong handshake from your devoted friend. Bear up and keep hoping for the best.

Naudinet

All this text was legibly written in tiny writing on a single postcard.

28 August 1916

Mother,

God and Destiny have spoken. However great the misfortune, we must submit to it, and even in this tragedy, which strikes at our deepest roots, we must screw up our courage and face the challenge.

The way I got the news was horrible. Mr Meuret thought I knew, and the first words of his letter were 'the death of your dear father … '. Dear Little Mum, imagine what I went through at the moment I read that! A spiritual wound like that is worse than the worst physical torture. Did I cry? No! My heart was too full for that. I could hope for no consolation among my companions, all more or less strangers to me.

An hour later I was on the road again for another all-night drive. Alone in my lorry, and trundling towards the front in the pitch dark, I cried and cried, still, though, refusing to believe that this horrible nightmare could be true.

If only I could have been pouring out my grief among you all … But no! There I was, alone and lost in the deep-blue night, with my heart bleeding among the mournful boom of the guns.

Thinking of you, Mother, how much I cried. Knowing you are suffering, so far from me and it's impossible to share your pain, to comfort you. Fortunately my sweet little Popo, my good grandfather and my poor grandmother are there with you, and the main thing is that I know how courageous you are, that you have a strong soul. This thought is a real relief for me.

Pierre, Paulette and Augusta in mourning, September 1916. (Private collection)

29 August 1916 (*continued on same sheet of paper*)

I've just got your letters, and they have helped to restore my courage now that I've got over the first shock. They were a motley collection: first one from Marraine[1] which, if I'd got it in time, would have prepared me well for the bad news. Grandpa's fine letter, full of courage and energy, was sent on the 7th, but didn't reach me until the 28th. It lifted my spirits a lot and reminded me again how I need to take it like a man. And then there was another lovely letter from Popo, which I kissed because it went straight to my heart. Tell her that she is a comfort to everyone in the house and I love her very much. Now more than ever I look forward to seeing you all again and hugging you all. When can it be, I wonder?

I finally had the pleasure of meeting Mr Naudinet. He had come out from France on the 12th and brought me news. We had a long chat, and I found him charming and very sympathetic.

All this has settled me down and, in accepting the inevitable, I have rediscovered the energy and enthusiasm which you need to cope with what life throws at you. The internal damage, like an internal wound, will take a long time to heal.

What a fine man Grandpa is! How much we love him and what a model he is for us all!

Recently, Mum, I have become aware that my childhood is quite at an end. Rocky though it is, life has opened before me, and I only await the end of this terrible war to set about fulfilling my ambitions.

---

1   His godmother, who occasionally sent correspondence and food parcels.

Little Mum, I've got to stop now, so I kiss you very tenderly, because I know my kisses are a comfort to you. These are my best and gentlest kisses, to lessen your pain, but even so you must save some of them for Popo, Grandma and Grandpa.

Your son looking forward keenly to the future,

Pierre

Towards the end of her life Paulette related to my mother the circumstances of her father's death: "He had been kicked in the head by a horse, and it caused a depressed fracture of the skull which put pressure on the brain. He suffered pain and nervous twitches on the opposite side of his body. Granted leave to return to Montauban, he was at first opposed to the idea of an operation; his doctor, however, persuaded him to allow what was considered to be a routine procedure, and he might as well take the opportunity. Louis, therefore, underwent a trepanning operation, but the surgeon, probing further than anticipated, punctured the dura mater layer of the brain, causing fluid to spread and Louis to relapse into a deep coma. Three days later, on August 4th, Louis died aged 45. His widow Augusta was 39."

Pierre was granted brief compassionate leave by the military authorities.

Two short postcards from Marseilles:

29 September 1916 (*his birthday*)

Dear Mum, It's five o'clock, and I am 20 years old. I kiss you tenderly on the neck. Tomorrow we embark on the slow boat 'Odessa', and it will no doubt be a long voyage.

Big hugs, and don't worry,

Pierre

4 October 1916

Set sail on the 'Admiral Obry'

6

It's real war, and I'm becoming an old savage again

P ierre was not the kind of man to grouse as soldiers often do, and it worried his mother when occasionally he would relate how hot or cold he was, or that he was not eating well. She was right to be concerned. The men were exhausted by the Macedonian summer heat, and in that weakened state fell victim to diseases such as malaria, dysentery, scurvy, malaria and swamp fever. "General Sarrail's office issued the following statistics of deaths by disease in the first half of 1916: in a total loss of 48,000 men, only 4,264 had fallen in actual combat. More than 2,000 had died in hospital, and 42,000 had been evacuated, of which 32,500 were cases of illness rather than wounding. The figures for the second half of the year were even worse, and all this in an army of only 130,000 men."[1]

General Sarrail[2] wrote to General Lyautey[3] on 16 December: "The Eastern Army, unlike those on the Western Front, has fought without intermission or relief. Swamp fever has run through the ranks of men weakened by excessive physical demands."[4]

With the arrival of winter, temperatures plummeted. Reaching minus 6 in Salonika, it was minus 10 to 15 degrees centigrade in the mountains, with heavy snow. In these conditions the men slept in tents. The roads were damaged by storms, creating severe difficulties for the lorry drivers transporting supplies. Letters from home arrived at irregular intervals. Some, carried in ships torpedoed in the Mediterranean, never arrived at all. Pierre had been granted compassionate leave following the death of his father. Given the circumstances, this was remarkable considering the journey length and prevailing conditions. It did him good, but one can only imagine what the other men in his section thought about it.

Most civilians back home had little idea what the Eastern Army was doing; this ignorance appears to have extended to the highest levels of government: Why were so many men committed for the purpose of creating a diversion to tie down German and Austrian troops? Georges Clemenceau contemptuously referred to them as the "gardeners of Salonika" (a reference to their entirely rational cultivation of vegetables to ward off scurvy). These soldiers were a "'forgotten army', whose suffering was due to the poor strategy and tactics of their commanders"; when in spite of this they went on to win decisive victories in the final months of the war, they received little credit.

Only a few of Pierre's letters, written on black bordered mourning notepaper, exist for the end of 1916. There were two in October, only one in November and three more in December. They are addressed from Sorovich[5] and Vakuskoy, small cantonments on the

---

1   Pierre Miquel, *Les Poilus d'Orient*, p. 253
2   General Maurice Sarrail (1856-1929). Commander Salonika front 1915-17.
3   General Louis Lyautey (1853-1934). French general famous for his colonial exploits, rather like Gordon of Khartoum, only more successful. [T's N]
4   Miquel, *Les Poilus d'Orient*, p.252
5   Now called Amyndeo or Aminteo, 20 miles south-east of Florina.

Monastir. (c.1910).

Sanitary service in Greece. Photo by Pierre Suberviolle (Private collection)

railway between Florina and Monastir. The contemporary map on the previous page shows these places; modern maps are difficult to use because so many place-names have changed. See also map in the introduction.

12 October 1916

Dear Little Mum,

Here I am back with the unit, and it's really good. We have advanced and are still advancing, now more than 120 miles from Salonika. We are billeted in the ruins of a little village which the Bulgarians have just abandoned.

It's real war here, Mum, so there is no time for moping, which is just as well because it was hard for me leaving France again.

The voyage was OK, with calm seas and no submarines, although there were 2000 of us on board, herded together and fed like cattle.

I finally got to Salonika on the 10th October, where I got the good news that we had gained ground. I made haste to rejoin my unit, which had advanced.

And now I'm back among the bare mountains and wonderful lakes, and turning back into an old savage among these dirty wretches who are more pro-Bulgar than pro-French. It feels like being in enemy territory, and my revolver and my knife are always to hand. I keep a good look out for myself, don't you worry! [6]

---

6   An extract from the *Journal of Military Operations* for October 1916 conveys an atmosphere of mutual hostility: "The cavalry, assisted or not by the Albanians, will take the area of Biklista, clear the area of all comitadjis and disarm all the inhabitants except Greek soldiers to be re-attached to their units. Isolated Greek solders should be disarmed, because there has been a recent case in Florina where the Greeks have had

Bulgarian POWs. Photos by Pierre
Suberviolle. (Private collection)

I got your parcels, two with the tinned food and two with the shirts, socks and
jumper. All very good and welcome, thank you.

Big hugs to you and everyone there,

Pierre

12 November 1916 (*to Paulette from Sorovich (Amindeo)*)

... we're back living like savages again, here more than ever. We are living like bears!
We're camped by a little lake surrounded by high snow-capped mountains. It's a
splendid sight, but unfortunately it is not very warm in our little tents: how I miss my
old bedroom at No. 34 Rue Emile Pouvillon! I wake up in the morning to find freezing
fog outside, and have to be quick to light my pipe to warm up the end of my nose! My
pipe draws like a steam engine, I can tell you, and its kiss is the only thing I have to
warm my heart!

Vakuskoy, 15 December 1916

Dear Little Mum,

I've just got your registered letter of 23rd November with the second money order.

---

to shoot a Bulgarian dressed in a Greek uniform." The comitadjis were nationalists rebelling against Serbs,
Greeks and Bulgarians. Biklishta, now Bilisht just inside Albania, is a few miles southwest of Monastir.

Postcard of Monastir, 1917. (Private collection)

That's a full 23 days it's taken to get here, but it was no less welcome for that, I assure you. A letter from my Mum is a real pleasure, but unfortunately rather a rare one. That's only the fourth I've got since I came back from leave, which is two letters a month. I don't complain, because when I get them your letters are so full of courage and tenderness that they keep my spirits up for a fortnight at a time. On the other hand you complain about my letters as well! I can see from your letter that quite a few of mine must not have arrived either. I have asked for several odds and ends, but you don't mention them.

There's nothing surprising about these delays. First of all several ships have recently been torpedoed, and with Bulgarians in front of us and Greeks behind us, communications with Salonika are less than perfect. Dear God! What a life!

Whatever happens, Mum, stay strong and brave, and even if my letters are sometimes late, be sure that you, Popo, Granny and Grandpa are always in my thoughts. When I'm alone in my tent I often kiss the photo of you and Paulette which I've had ever since I went off to be a soldier.

As I told you, we're at Vakuskoy not far from Mo ... and things are much the same. Always loads of work to do, and now with a musical accompaniment provided by the Bulgars, who have brought up an Austrian gun and are letting fly at us with a few big whoppers.

Apart from that I'm still in good health, though my manners are descending into barbarism. The weather is pretty cold, so I've got my pipe out again. I'd love you to send me a really BIG ROPP pipe [a well-known brand of French pipes]. I don't care what shape it is (but don't tell Grandpa that!).

Let's speak of home matters. I was pleased to hear that the helper managed your business well. Dear Grandpa must husband his resources so that he survives in good health until his grandson comes back to replace him.

There is one thing that is cheesing me off (if you'll excuse the slang); it is you saying that you're doing all the housework yourself. Little Mum, you mustn't on any account do that. **I don't approve!**

Don't tell me that you are hard up! You must employ a maid even if it means cutting down on the money you send out here, and I shall be cross if you don't. You will wear yourself out with the housework, if indeed you haven't already done so.

Also, Mum, think of little Popo and me and ease up on yourself so that you can go on being our dear Mum. If you overwork you will get ill. You will grow old so that when I come home from the war I shan't want to kiss you any more, so Look Out!

I hope that Grandpa is telling you the same thing, and I'm pretty sure he is, because he will be the first to complain if you don't follow your big boy's advice.

I leave you now with a big kiss (provided you do what I tell you) and asking for you to write more often.

Big hugs for everyone,

Pierre

17 January 1917

Mademoiselle my little sister,

Your little soldier is miserable. The snow is still falling outside, which shuts out the sound of the guns, and creates a glacial silence. Little Pierre, curled up in a ball under his blanket with his pipe under his nose, reflects that life in war time is not a bed of roses.

The snow was pretty, dear Popo, when we used to watch it out of the window of the nice warm study, as it covered the branches of the yew tree or fell on the flower beds in the garden. Here, by God, we wish it would go to Hell! If you were here I could put some snow in your neck, in the hope that by teasing you I should forget the cold. How does that strike you, little Kid?

Oh! 'Little Kid'! What am I saying? I see your eyes widening as you get ready to box my ears, but I'm not there any more across the table, and when I tease you there is nothing to fear.

You see I want to poke fun at you to wind you up a bit tonight.

Are you still playing the coquette with your face powdered with rice? I'm sure you do! Now that you are a young lady, have you abandoned your short skirts for ones which don't show your knees? Do you still gossip with your girl-friends?

Quick, a big hug and I'm off, because now I can see Mother making big eyes at me!

Pierre

P.S. *My little sister, I kiss your beautiful blue eyes* (written in English)

A chart drawn by Pierre at the close of this letter:
– temperature: –10°C + wind, snow
– health: all right
– morale: still rather good except for periods of blues
– needed: not much, except for letters
Hugs for Mum, Grandpa and Grandma

20 January 1917

Dear Little Mum,

Your big son is braver than you, because here is a long letter. Will you reply to it? You wrote a word on Paulette's letter, surely to tease me? You know that your letters are the ones I want most and which I read with the greatest pleasure. Most letters like these are just trifles, and the effect of them soon wears off, but yours, written with such a tender regard for your big boy, are irreplaceable. How long is it since I had a word from you?

Will and energy alone keep us going. News of loved ones is vital to counter the effects of pain and exhaustion. One needs courage to drive away the depressive feelings which are never far away.

On the bright side I have just received :

The registered letter dated Christmas Day with the 150 francs.

A delightful letter from Popo written on January 3rd.

Two little parcels which I really enjoyed. You spoiled me with the liqueurs, the cake and the tins of food which, trust me, we wolfed down. Perhaps we deserved it. Thank you, too, for the 100 franc note: you know that always comes in handy.

A bit of gossip about me. We are still in the same area without a moment's rest, and with the bloody snow and freezing cold, and yet I'm still perfectly well. The only thing bothering me is that my pipes are all worn out, and I'm still waiting impatiently for the one I asked you for. Apart from that, nothing new, and time is dragging and dragging.

How's it going with the household business? Is Grandpa happy with his assistant? I hear you've had more problems with the Delage. Is little Popo still well-behaved? Are my pipes still tidily arranged in my bedroom? And most of all, little Mum, have you taken my advice and looked after yourself?

Write to me! Write long letters so that I can enjoy a few moments with you! When I am depressed and all on my own, I dream of days gone by, yes, but when I read your letters it seems a more present reality, as if you were there by me.

Your big boy who doesn't love you a bit ...

Pierre

P.S. can you please send me twenty flints and a big length of wick-tinder[7], about three metres of it, as thick as in this sketch.

28 January 1917

It was four days before I could finish the letter and send it off. So much the better, because I am the happiest soldier in the world! What was in my Mum's parcel?

A PIPE! And what a beauty! A proper old soldier's pipe! You can't imagine how much that means to me! It is perfect in every detail: its bowl is big and thick, the wood is top-quality and the design is amazing. In a word, it's a dream! Mum, your big kid hugs you in thanks. And what else was in the parcel! An authentic *galantine*[8] from the Viguiers and Surviolles, with their wonderful quince jam and so on. If you'd only seen us tucking into it you would've been really happy. The battery is also working well, so I am fully equipped.

---

7   Used to light Pierre's tobacco pipe. [T's N]
8   Galantine: A typical southwest duck or goose pâté. [T's N]

11 February 1917

Dear Little Mum,

Thanks for your long letter and the 100 franc money order. I really enjoyed reading your letter over and over again, because it is such a long time since I have had that pleasure.

What you say about Marie-Antoinette did not surprise me. I have been expecting such news for a long time. I have not had anything from Mr Barthe; if I have a minute I will write to him. I will send him a copy of the letter (neither yes nor no, let's not beat about the bush).

Nothing much new, still bloody cold and loads of work to do, and recently we have had poison gas again. It doesn't bother me; I keep smoking my pipe and don't notice.

Big hugs,

Pierre

What was going on with Marie-Antoinette? It looks as if Pierre has written to her in secret!

26 February 1917 (*a facsimile of this letter, written on an envelope, is printed in the Introduction*)

Dear Little Mum,

Nothing new except that the cold is appalling. We have got snow up to our chests and it is really difficult to get the lorries moving along the roads. I am well covered up, Mum, so don't worry about that. I have got everything I need and I am in good health. Write to me often because this war is dragging on, and the longer it goes on the worse it is.

Loving hugs,

Pierre

11 March 1917

You wouldn't believe what we are having to put up with. There is more than a metre of snow on the ground and it was between −15 C° and −20 C° degrees every day in February. Now on the other hand the thaw has set in and the rains have come, so in my wretched little tent I am soaking wet day and night. Happily when I wake up in the night to find everything frozen, a little sip of China-China[9] puts everything right and I am soon snoring again ...

24 March 1917

Dear Mum,

I am feeling better already. Today is the first day of my treatment, but what treatment! You need to be brave, and you know I am.

In the morning a shower and a wash, or rather scrubbing the whole body with a scratchy brush and black soap. After that when the pimples are really itchy you have to put some sulphur cream on them, which really burns. I had to sing at the top of my voice whilst scrubbing myself so that I didn't scream out. I hope that tomorrow it will be less painful: they say the first day is the worst. I certainly scrubbed as hard as I could

---

9   A kind of liqueur. [T's N]

Vehicles operating in snowy conditions in Macedonia. (*Lectures pour tous*, 15 February 1916)

so that I would get better faster. Apart from that life is okay. I took advantage of the afternoon to study some History because they want that at Fontainebleau[10]. I found it easier to remember than it used to be.

Yesterday evening I had just finished writing my letter to Popo when we had a visit from the Gothas[11]. Lovely evening! Lots of noise, lots of lights in the sky and rather less fun, the bombs falling around us.

But that is war.

Deep down I am not too bothered to be here: apart from the damned itching, it would be quite a nice rest. My life as an instructor over the last few days is hardly taxing. I leave you now with a big hug.

Pierre

Are some letters missing? This one contains several mysteries. What illness is he suffering from? What is the "itching"? Is it perhaps scabies? Where is he? He is an instructor but what does he instruct in? Whatever may be, he found the time to write to Mr Barthe, Marie-Antoinette's father. He made a copy of the letter for his mother:

25 March 1917
My dear Sir,

It has been a long time that I have wanted to write to you in reply to your pleasant letter, and here at last is an opportunity.

---

10   Fontainebleau was home to the reserve officers' school where Pierre was applying.
11   *Gotha* G.V: Heavy bomber employed by the *Luftstreitkräfte* (German Army Air Service) during the First World War.

Your letter found me beyond the frontiers of Greece and Serbia (A ... ... .a)[12] just as the advance was beginning. Since then there has not been a spare moment even to scribble a few lines. What you said in your letter was too serious for me to do other than reply frankly.

First of all I must apologise for my childish behaviour. Simple good sense and sober reflection have made me see the justice of your point of view. Indeed to be absolutely frank the same reasoning had long deterred me from beginning a correspondence with Marie-Antoinette. I was indeed very young and too far away to make a commitment so hastily. Gloomy thoughts of what might happen to me also held me back and these thoughts were justified by the subsequent death of my poor father. This reminded us all of life's uncertainty.

The best and only excuse that I can offer you is my soldier's heart. This has indeed been my main support in the face of sufferings, and it even allows us to laugh in the face of death.

At the beginning these horrible things caused us to feel the good old French patriotism. Since then a lot of water has gone under the bridge, and these early feelings have somewhat lost their force. Each man now fights for his own dream, and is happy enough to sacrifice his skin for a person or an idea which he reveres. Only listening to my heart and dreaming of the future, you can appreciate, my dear sir, what has been for me the ideal which has kept me going through all this.

Such is my confession and I hope it will earn your forgiveness.

I shall look forward anxiously to your reply. You have my solemn word as a soldier that I will content myself with memories and hopes, and give up secret correspondence.

I shall be very pleased my dear sir, to put this matter behind us. Your sincere and warm friendship is a great comfort to my mother and me. You know, too, how much I have always valued your opinion and advice. I am going to need them even more in the time to come.

Please accept my dear sir this testimony to my deepest and heartfelt goodwill.

P. Suberviolle

Here is the letter of Mr Barthe's which had provoked Pierre's response above:

Brétigny, 12 February 1917

My dear friend,

It is a fortnight since I visited Montauban at the end of my leave and visited your house. It was a long time since I had seen your family. It was nice to find them all in good health, and as you can imagine we spoke a lot about you. It was nice to read some of your letters, and the affectionate tone you used towards all those who wait for your return there. I noticed as well that you are full of courage and acceptance of your lot. I can congratulate you on your big heart. Your mother was anxious to give me your address and to have me promise to write to you; and in any case I had already decided to share with you certain observations which I made to her and your grandfather.

We had discovered that you had written several secret letters to Marie-Antoinette. This was an inexcusable and childish action and I must speak frankly to you about it.

---

12   Almost certainly Albania.

You are sensible enough to know that in the present situation there is absolutely no point in trying to fix any project for the future. It is going to be a long time before either of you can enter into any kind of engagement.

I would also point out that although the risks for you are relatively small, among us that is not the case. Marie-Antoinette must remain completely free, because I don't want her to wait many years in expectation and then be cast into a depression which may cast a shadow over her whole future. I don't think I need to go on and on about this to make you understand and accept that it is absolutely essential to avoid creating expectations which may never come to anything.

When I made these points to your mother, she was upset. Her love for you blinds her to some extent. Some days afterwards she recognised that I had been completely justified in my view. I am sure it will be the same with you, because you too are sensible and good hearted. I count on your good sense that you will forget about all this until your age and situation make it realistic to start thinking along these lines.

You on your part can count on my sincere affection and regard for your welfare. Write to me now and again. I shall be glad to know that you are not in distress, and to help you with my advice.

We have all been back here together for more than a month. It has been bitterly cold (−15 to −18 degrees) and our house isn't really made for this. When shall we see the banks of the Garonne again? Not too long we hope.

Until then, with my very warmest good wishes,

Antonin Barthe

15 April 1917

Dear Little Mum,

How long is it now since your big son had any news? Can you guess? It's now been a whole month since I had a single word from you, Popo, Grandpa or anyone!

So what is going on? It must surely be the postal service, because you love me too much to make me miserable by leaving me so long without news. I'm sorry to say that I am very miserable at the moment, and the only solution will be to get one of your lovely letters full of love for your big lad. The last letter I got from you (with the 100 franc money order) was dated 28 February, and I got it on 13 March. I sent an acknowledgement for it, and the two parcels, straight back.

On the 21st I sent a long letter to Grandpa. On the 23rd I sent you a note with the letter from Mr Barthe and my reply. On 1st April I wrote to Popo thanking her for the other two parcels. On Easter Day I wrote a long letter to you. I'm sorry if it was a bit soppy, but I was going through a very bad patch that day.

I reckon that I should have had replies to the first two letters by now, and whether they come today or tomorrow or the next day I shall be very glad to have them as I am very down at the moment.

Oh Mum, write soon and write often. When we are far apart, and I am lost and alone, cut off from all contact with the world, a letter is like a kiss or caress which gives my soul back a little of the affection which it misses so much. It gives me courage and good spirits. Exchanging letters makes it possible for our souls to speak to each other, and I can imagine that I'm there with you again.

Dear Mum, don't make me suffer. Send me more letters, which are the only thing

Augusta and Paulette. (Private collection)

that can lift my spirits. Then once again I can write back with a light heart and send you really big hugs.

A bit about me. As I said before in a letter some time ago, we spent some time in A ... ... a, but now we're back round M ... ... , and as the war is still going on nothing much is different, but I'm due for a bit of rest; our equipment is completely worn out and we shall be pulled back for repairs.

The main change has been in the weather. A week ago we had snow, but now the summer has begun, and here we are in shirtsleeves and pith helmets. I'm keeping going, not too tired and free from fever, and if I could shake off my feelings of depression everything would be fine.

What's going on with you at home? Just a word would bring back memories, and I want to know about everything. These days, Mum, I'm fighting for our home rather than for France. When I think of home, I think of you all there together. I imagine Grandpa slaving away on behalf of his little grandson, Popo quite a grown-up sweet young lady, Grandma doing her work and you doing four people's work to keep everything in order; then I think of my bedroom with all my bits and pieces and my pipes arranged in a row.

Oh Mum, promise to keep in touch with lots and lots of news, and I shall send you lots of big hugs, and I send you one now and another for everyone there.

Pierre

P.S. Could you send me the two pairs of khaki shorts I had last year, and some socks? I don't need any shirts, but I should like a really enormous pipe (a ROPP or a G.B.D.), but don't tell Grandpa I'm having a curved one!

Obviously the postal service was not working well: several letters which Pierre mentions were not in the collection, and to add to his sense of deprivation from the lack of letters from home, he was forbidden to write to Marie-Antoinette!

For May and June there are a few short letters written from Sakuleno, near Vakuskoy, and from a place which seems to be called Krunjam.

Sakuleno, 28 May 1917
Dear Little Mum,

Not much time to write. I'm standing in for the Quartermaster for the whole unit, because he's in Salonika on leave. All day long I'm busy with orders and stock-checks. I am managing to get through it pretty well although I've never done that kind of thing before. When you set your mind to something you can generally master it, eh, Mum?

Nothing much else has changed. Always the sun beating down, my same little canvas tent and my usual group of mates. Good health and spirits. Since I had the last two letters, Popo's with the 200 francs and yours, nothing again for several days.

Big hugs,
Pierre

Sakuleno, 29 May 1917
Dear Popo,

Nothing new here, just waiting and waiting for ever.

Memo: dear Mademoiselle my sister, you are requested to write to me frequently. If you disobey this order you will be punished: I shall never hug you again!

Salonika, 16 July 1917
Dear Little Mum,

You can't be serious! Which of us is the more crazy? I'm not really complaining, my dear Mum, it's just that I feel like pulling your leg a bit tonight because I am so happy. Your long letter of 18th June has just arrived!

It's nine o'clock in the evening, and the sweltering heat of the day has finally finished. One by one the stars are coming out and taking their positions in the sky. The sky is such a deep blue that it makes me think of things far, so far away, and of infinity.

Yes, Mum, here is your little Pierre, with his big pipe in his mouth, stretched out on the grass with his eyes glued to your letter. He can't read it any more because it has gone dark, but what does it matter? He already knows it by heart, and clasping it in his hands he feels himself closer, almost in contact with those he loves.

Another vision presents itself before him. Is that perhaps a sultana among the mulberry trees, against the minaret which is the only remaining smudge of white in the darkness? Allah, have you perhaps allowed one of your beautiful Houris[13] to escape from Paradise?

---

13   According to the Koran, *Houris* are virgins in Paradise.

But what do I see? The vision becomes clearer. God, <u>how beautiful she is, how chic and graceful</u>! <u>Is she the perfect woman</u>? I can't take my eyes off her, but gradually the moon rises and peeps over the crest of Mount Ortiac. And Oh! Tragedy! My beautiful Houri, horrified no doubt by my impertinent regard, is returning to the land of dreams.

Now Pierre angrily sucks at his pipe which, in his reverie, he has allowed to go out! He sinks back down from the sixth heaven into the real world below. Holy Sun of the East! After eighteen months have you not perhaps touched my brain?

But dear Mum let me get back to your letter. After the passage which I have underlined above, I think of what you concluded: "If I was going to subject your heart to torture I wouldn't dare to say any more and should stop here". No, Mum, you haven't upset me. How can I explain it to you? Your letter makes me happy and sad at the same time. But this sadness isn't all that bad, as it is more like a melancholy, with a certain sweet charm.

It was good to hear about the visit of the Barthe family. You think as highly of them as I do, and so you suffered by their being so far away. Their good and open friendship will always be a comfort to you.

Now Mum, let's be frank with one another: Yes, I love her, and it is the hope that my dream and yours will come true which stiffens my resolve to follow the path I have marked out, as I promised you.

It is this vision of future happiness, which will be a great joy for you, which guides my thoughts. This love is planted deep within me, so it enables me, or forces me to follow your wishes: why should I not listen to what it is telling me? Only the realisation of this vision will make me happy when I am back at home working alongside Grandpa again. All my future depends on it, for what is life without happiness? In that word I include all the joys of family life, the pleasure of seeing one's dreams and ambitions realised, and the feeling that one has not lived on earth in vain.

It may be that I cannot have all these things. I know that life is beset with a thousand difficulties. Even if many of our hopes go unfulfilled, if just one of them comes true it may do duty for all the others and supply that reason for living. One must live life, and one only lives it once.

That's the end of the serious bit. Ouch! I re-light my pipe and get back to chat. The main thing is that you should not be jealous. I know you, Mum. If I say anything too hasty you will as sure as Hell come back with 'Oh Pierre, I don't want you loving anyone else but your Mum!' You know I'm right, and I can see you smiling (in my memory, because we've already been through it!)

Now, because you know all my thoughts, here are some serious ones. Please don't put your foot in it by saying too much, and don't make any commitments. Time is short, and a lot is happening. Destiny is at hand: we only need to follow it while guiding it as best we can.

I stop now, little Mum, and give you a big hug.

P. Suberviolle

P.S. Tomorrow I'll write again about ordinary business, parcels I've had, how my health is, the weather and all that.

This is one of the few letters which Pierre signed "Suberviolle"; the writing paper for this correspondence, and all subsequent letters until the following September, was in black-edged mourning paper.

Salonika, 19 July 1917

Dear little Mum,

What must you have thought of me when you read the letter I sent you two days ago? It's the sort of thing that happens when you spend a long time out here. I await your reply with interest.

Today I'm writing about all the things that interest you, and I'm going to go through your last three letters and reply in greater detail than I have up to now. I loved your letter of 20 May, where you tried to raise my spirits. Do you think I have lost my courage? Remember that whatever was going on, my heart was always French. Unfortunately it is so depressing here, and the life so hard, that it is impossible to avoid being down some of the time. Leaving that aside, I'll write a letter to Grandpa one of these days telling him the inside story of the "Eastern Army."

In the midst of all this there is only one thing I really need, and you know what that is: a letter from my Mum, always so good and loving that it wipes out the memory of the bad times.

Besides that, it's party-time when the parcels arrive. I was waiting for one particular one for a long time, and then dear Mum, what joy when the pipe finally arrived! Smoking is one of the only pleasures we have, and most of us here would sooner lose an arm than our pipe! I also very much appreciated the sausages and the cigars from Etienne, which arrived at a very fortunate moment. I was just off on a 180 mile drive into Albania, in a single vehicle and on duty, so my mate and I had an excuse to scoff the lot between us!

One of these days when I'm feeling lyrical I'll tell you the full story of that drive. The top and bottom of it is that when I finally got to Lake Presba, in the savage beauty of the Albanian countryside, I was the happiest of men. After a fine meal of half of the sausage, wreathed in the smoke of fine French cigars, I dreamed of you all.

Salonika, 5 August 1917

Dear Popo,

I was very happy to get your kind little note. First many congratulations for your success. Ten prizes[14] is fantastic! I never managed that myself! How proud of you everyone at home must be!

It amused me to think of you studying for your Bac[15]. Will you be plunging into Latin with Mr. Cambon? Don't let it get you down!

Have you thought that it might help Mum more if you went to Grandma Nini to learn how to make pâtés and cakes? It might make your husband happier later on, too (I'm hoping that you aren't thinking of becoming a nun!). Either way, kid, you can please yourself.

Nothing much new in my life. Everything's peaceful. When are we going to be

---

14   Ten prizes: This means that she excelled in ten subjects during the past year, and had been awarded books as prizes. [T's N]

15   French school exam equivalent to A level. [T's N]

relieved? I'm looking forward to setting foot in lovely France again, seeing you all and hugging you tight.

I was quite unaware of Mr. Cavayé's illness. Is it a fever? We've all either had one or will probably get one.

For myself, everything's fine.

I hug you,

Pierre

10 August 1917 (*to his sister*)

Do you know how many letters I've had from you since the beginning of June?
- Mum's of 18th June
- Yours of 22nd
- Grandma Nini's of 29th
- Yours of 20th July
- Your latest one of 1st August

That's five letters in a month and a half.

25 August 1917

Dear Little Mum,

A little chat with you, which I hope you'll like. Surely you will, you probably worried about me, the fact is that I was moved again.

Let me update you on where I've been. Remember that our unit was pulled out of the line and back to Salonika for repairs and maintenance at the beginning of July? We all got back, and it was good to see the city again, but no sooner had we arrived than they started to allocate drivers to other units, thus breaking up our team. The trouble is they need good drivers who know the area, and we've got plenty of them. I've had to watch my mates disappearing one by one. Now there are only a few of us old ones left with a bunch of new guys, which is a pain. I could have got a posting myself, but I hung on hoping for something better to turn up.

To keep myself from boredom and melancholy I got myself attached to a repair workshop. I enjoyed myself for nearly a month living like a manual worker, learning how to do all the repairs to the vehicles. I even learned how to file and forge metals.

Then the posting I had my eye on came up. I finished off in the workshop, and a week later I took up my new job as the chauffeur of the officer commanding the transport services of the French Eastern Army.

And here I am, the driver of the big boss. I have two vehicles which only I am allowed to drive: one is a 6-cylinder Schneider, and the other a 10-HP Panhard. The captain is one of our bravest, very distinguished and a charming man of the world.

I am really pleased to have this job for a number of reasons (and there were plenty of other blokes who wanted it!) – first of all with the daily contact with the captain, who chats the whole time we are driving along. I have benefitted a lot from these conversations, which can't be said of most barrack room chat.

Apart from that I have had the pleasure of driving the length and breadth of Greece and Macedonia. Since I am completely at his disposition, nobody else bothers me at all, so no more guard duties, and no more fatigues! On the whole, Mum, I think I'm on a winner here, as I'm sure you will agree!

The great fire of Salonika. (*Le Miroir*, 16 September 1917)

As to other matters I should mention the big fire at Salonika. I'll tell you all about that in my next letter.

I'm still waiting for your letter, but I don't complain because all the post is taking time to come through. When I left Salonica the July money order had still not arrived, so you can claim the money back for that one and the June one from the Post Office. I'm still waiting for the parcel with the clothes in: khaki shirts and shorts, towels, socks and flints for my lighter.

Apart from that nothing new. I'm waiting impatiently for my relief[16]. Health still good.

Big hugs,
Pierre

16 September 1917
Dear Popo,

I hope you'll like these photos which I've had taken. Although they are not top quality, you will recognise little Pierre in his summer kit.

I hope I shall soon be with you. I'm gambling everything on it. Nothing else much new apart from the fantastic journeys I've been on. I'll tell you all about them when I can.

After you get this letter, don't send any more parcels to me, because I shall be gone by the time they arrive. You can still write, though.

Big hugs,
Pierre

16   Relief i.e., Pierre was awaiting a period of rest and recuperation prior to his next posting. [T's N]

Pierre at Florina 1917. (Private collection)

Florina 1917. Photo by Pierre
Suberviolle. (Private collection)

Serbian music sheet. (Private collection)

Sadly we hear nothing further about the fire at Salonika or the magnificent drives round Greece. Pierre evidently saved these stories for his forthcoming leave, due in October. All that remains is a map on which he marked all his journeys (see a photo of this map on page xx). This verifies that he had been to the Albania coast opposite Corfu, and right down to the Gulf of Corinth in the south. He also visited Delphi and Athens, as recounted many years later to one of his nephews, who had just returned from a camping trip to Greece. He also jokingly referred to another "souvenir" – malaria, from which he suffered recurrent bouts for the remainder of his life. Another souvenir, packed into his return luggage, was a collection of Serbian music sheets. Pierre was a skilled violinist, although he remains silent about this in his correspondence. For a pictorial witness to his journeys, we also have stacks of retail postcards – perhaps there was no film available for his pocket Kodak.

7

My childhood is over

As 1917 came to an end, the war on the Western Front continued in bloody stalemate. The vaunted Nivelle Offensive (16 April-9 May), in which France placed all its hopes to drive the entrenched invader from its soil, ended in bloody disappointment. The consequent internal unrest that all but crippled the French Army was followed by official measures to improve troop morale and fighting capacity. Moreover, in another event of international significance, the Bolshevik Revolution elevated Lenin to power.

Pierre's final letter from Macedonia was dated 27 September. Following this, he departed Salonika for one month's home leave, disembarking at Marseilles. He entrained for Paris on or about 12 November:

Paris, the 12th
Dear Little Mum,

Before I go to dinner I must send you a word about the journey. It went very smoothly and here I am, even though a little sad, in Paris.

I won't attempt to hide the fact that yesterday evening I had a very heavy heart, but meeting Marie-Antoinette perked me up no end. The result is that alongside the normal doleful feelings I am able to dream of something better. You will guess what it is, but I'm not saying anything else.

I hadn't been able to see them during the trip, and it wasn't until we got to Austerlitz that I was able to shake them by the hand and to feast my eyes (and heart) on Marie-Antoinette, who looked sweet and charming. I can see you starting to laugh, Mum, and Grandpa too: the lucky devil was able to give her a hug, whereas I am forbidden![1]

I will stop now, Mum, and will write more this evening as I said I would. Just now I need to say that I am once again bowled over by Paris! I'm not sure exactly where I am at this minute, it's some café in some square, but goodness knows where! I'm going to wander off now and find a nice restaurant, and when I've eaten I shall take a taxi to where Mr. Leclainche and Paul live. At the end of the evening I shall set off for Versailles. No point in going on the town: I've had a wild enough time on leave!

Big kisses, and I'll write again this evening.

Pierre

3 December 1917
Dear Little Mum,

It's my first day, and to get properly signed in I've been shoved around from pillar to post in the office of the 20th squadron. I should really say 'offices', as I had to present

---

1   Marie-Antoinette refers to this episode in her memoirs: "During these four years of war, we had only seen each other twice, at Brétigny and in Montauban railway station, when he was going to the front and we were going to Paris. My father did not allow him to travel with us. Thus a few hours of happiness were lost at a time when they were so rare."

107

Letter posted from Terminus Hotel, Versailles. (Private collection)

myself at three different counters and answer the same questions three times. Finally I managed to make them understand that, after 20 months in Orient, I'd been assigned to Versailles. I'd gone in at 8.00 a.m. and finally emerged at 3.00 p.m. attached to Section 520 of the Officer Selection organisation. It's been a full day!

That's not all. I've got two more hurdles to cross, as I've got to deal with the Central Vehicle Office and then the S.P. 550. When that's done I hope to be able to join the Seventh Army.

I still haven't had time to see the Colonel Loths. I shall try and go there tomorrow morning so that I can get out of here as fast as I can.

Nothing remarkable about life at Versailles. The accommodation is unfit for human habitation, so we've been given leave to sleep overnight in the town, where I've done well to find a room. Write to me at the hotel until further notice. Nothing else to say because there is nothing else to say!

Big, big hugs,

Pierre

Versailles, 4 December 1917

Dear Little Mum,

Nothing much to say today. It has been a very quiet day, though we had a medical inspection this morning. Apart from that, nothing. I am counting on leaving these barracks tomorrow or the day after to go to the S.P. 500. This is the only place I can sort things out for my departure.

You can't imagine the chaos which reigns here. It's impossible to know what to do or where to go! I've bumped into quite a lot of old friends who have been able to get me out of several unpleasant duties. It's a classic of life behind the lines.

The confusion has at least the advantage of stopping me sinking into morbid thoughts, but it is unpleasant to get back into the dirty business. People say that we still have a long way to go. At the moment we are sending a lot of drivers to the Americans, and if I were not hoping to go with the 7th Army I would have asked to go with them because, Mum, I have changed my attitude from when I was on leave. Coming back from the East and wearing civilian clothes went to my head and made me do very stupid things.

I've just crossed Paris again and lived its life again. After such a long time without seeing it I have been able to experience and form an estimate of many things; but far from confirming my illusions, this demolished them one by one. Mum, I think I'm on the road to recovery and getting back to a healthier state of mind, just as you always advise. But let the cure take effect. I shall keep you abreast of my thinking, and for now I just list the three things which have made the difference:

Firstly, I've spent a long time thinking about what Mr. Massip said to me before I came back from leave.

Secondly, *Marie-Antoinette*.

Thirdly, the memory of a month of family life, which I appreciate the more since I came back to this hell again. Big hugs,

Pierre

5 December 1917

Dear Little Mum,

At last, this morning, something new. Here I am at Section 550 of the personnel selection. I can sort myself out a posting to the 7th Army.

But let's not speak of that. First I had the pleasure of meeting Durand, one of my two old mates at Dunkirk. We had kept together right up to the time I set sail for Salonika. It is great to find good old comrades again, and as a result I'm much less depressed than usual coming back from leave.

When I was home on leave you really made me drink too much wine, and I was left with hardly a pennyworth of common sense! This morning, straight after roll-call, I slipped away to avoid being taken for duty.

What should I do? At 8.00 I went for a quiet walk in the park[2]. The sun was hardly up. The park, still sleeping, showed itself in its full glory. No-one else out walking, and no outrageously dressed ladies in that park haunted by long-gone beauties. I felt a pure artistic pleasure in looking at the park all covered in frost, and I could dream to my heart's content in front of these immortal statues, which were fortunate enough to be made of stone.

Yes, life goes on and everything comes to an end. Only memories remain and even they soon dissolve. What do people struggle for, but for some grand and noble goal benefitting society or one's family? What is the point of money, leading us to an artificial life of luxury, or of debauchery, that leaves bitterness and bad memories? I am beginning to understand that a home, and a life of the mind (with the essential material foundation) are the only things that can bring satisfaction and a joy in living. Whoops! I'll stop here! Don't show this to anyone or they'll think I've had a touch of the sun out East!

Big hugs,
Pierre

Pierre thought for a while that he was going to be posted to Italy; then he sent this telegram:

Telegraph an order for 200 francs to the Fujol Hotel[3], 6, Rue Carnot, Versailles – Letter follows – Pierre

---

2   Evidently the garden of Versailles palace. [T's N]
3   The building, now a restaurant, remains. [T's N]

7 December 1917

Thank you Mum for the 200 francs, which arrived this afternoon. I wish I hadn't asked for them, as they have made me very unhappy. What's going on? Whichever of you it was (whether you or Grandpa) did not even enquire why I might have made such a request, but has hastily said 'Yes, here is the money, but this is the last time we will do it'. No message, or nice greeting or even some indication of why you are so angry.

My heart is very heavy, and writing this I am crying like a kid.

I shall stop now, Mum: don't think badly of me for writing so little, as I am too unhappy to write more.

Pierre

16 December 1917

Dear Little Mum,

Here I am again in the Vosges, and not in Italy at all! To avoid being sent there I feigned illness on the day we were supposed to go. My fever was already on record, so I was unable to go! I therefore had a few days to myself with the officer commanding the vehicle park. This went so well that on the 12th a special order arrived directing me to the place I wanted to be.

I have just this moment written to the commander to tell him I've got here. I don't want to waste time getting my future sorted out. I'm looking forward to this because I am really down at the moment. How hard it is getting back to the life of a soldier again!

The conditions on the front line are worse here than at Salonika. We are snowed in and it is bitterly cold. I think you would regret how much you went on at me during my leave if you could see me now.

I still haven't had any letters, and I am looking forward to them a lot, I can assure you. Write to me at T.M. 402 – B.C.M. Paris.[4]

Big hugs,
Pierre

18 December 1917

Dear Little Mum,

I've finally got to where I'm supposed to be. It's not much fun, I can tell you. Here's my definite address: 402 T.M. – B.C.M. Paris.

Now, please, as quickly as you can, send me at least 100 francs. I really need them and shall be in big trouble if I haven't a penny in my pocket. OK, OK, you'll go on at me, but I can't help that. I had 150 francs pinched from me on the day before I left Paris. Even the best men are sometimes caught out, I regret to say. If I hadn't gone on the officer training course I'd have had nothing to tell you about. Our mess bill is 20 francs a day and office expenses. If I could find a cheap room I'd take it to make my work easier.

You'll find it hard to credit this, but I am in a little village tucked away in the Vosges and eaten up with remorse over what happened on leave. I was very stupid and let myself be carried away too easily. Mum, I solemnly promise you that my childish behaviour is at an end. I'm going to put everything into getting a commission, either as an officer or (more likely because of my age) an under-officer[5]. It's the end of my career

---

4   TM 402 was a material transport section in the DSA, TP being personnel transport sections.
5   Under-officer: A non-commissioned officer. [T's N]

as a party animal!

Be sure to tell Grandpa to keep his spirits up and think of me from time to time. He is a good man at heart.

I love Marie-Antoinette, and I shall become a vet first because that's what you want, and also so that I can marry her.

I don't know what I can say to make you believe that I am sincere in all this. It hurts me to write to you, because I feel that you have lost confidence in me. Believe that I love you very much. Keep this letter, so that if I ever wander off the straight and narrow again (but that won't happen) you can quote it back at me to put me right!

A big hug, Mum, from your big son who is growing into a man and beginning to understand what life is and should be about.

Pierre

As to the money, send it by telegraph as quickly as you can to the address I gave you. I can assure you that I really need it.

Pierre dreamed of becoming a pilot, but, either because he recognised there was little chance of achieving this, or because his family insisted, he instead enrolled in a university science course at Toulouse just before the outbreak of war. Following the death of his father he would be expected to take over his veterinary practice.[6] Moreover, it appears that Marie-Antoinette's father was in league with the Suberviolles: Pierre could not "have Marie-Antoinette" unless he agreed to become a veterinarian. On arrival at veterinarian school he was asked "Why have you chosen to be a vet?" – His pithy reply? – "They made me."

19 December 1917

Dear Mum,

It takes guts to do this officer training. It's very hard work and particularly mastering military manoeuvres, which I've never had anything to do with.

Tough though it is I've got to go through with it. By writing to you I build up the resources of will and energy to persevere. I'm OK on the use and upkeep of vehicles, because I already knew what they told me. There's just the military rule-book and I think I'll cope with that.

I plan to stay here until the end of January, after we have the exam. We'll really need to pull big strings for me to pass, given how young I am. Therefore I'll do my best to study extra hard so they will notice me a bit, and I hope it will be all right with the commander.

Mum, keep writing me long letters to give me courage. I need them, and although I've only just started here I sometimes want to send the whole lot to hell.

I've decided to work, and I'll stick with it.

Bitter cold here with snow, but I'm not having too bad a time of it. Could you send the rest of my things: shirt, shorts, handkerchief, towel, shoes, big socks, and a canvas handbag. Also my box of compasses which is in the drawer of my bedside table.

Did you get my letter from yesterday asking for money? I'm up against it.

Bye, Mum, and big hugs,

Pierre

---

6   Run by Pierre's grandfather during the war years.

20 December 1917

Dear Little Mum,

I am feeling pretty good this evening. This afternoon an officer questioned me on my knowledge of vehicles, and although I haven't attended his lectures I got almost every answer right. He was amazed! His course has been going on for three weeks and the formal test is due in a few days. If that was all there was I should be sure of qualifying first time, but unfortunately there are also the military and paperwork aspects, which are a different kettle of fish. Commandant Arboux advised me to enrol on the second course in the first three weeks of January, so I'm going to do that. They run one course a month, and I hope I'll make it through in January. I also astonished them by my knowledge of vehicle maintenance, which is down to my time spent in the workshops in Salonika. At least I've been able to suggest that I'm not completely useless!

So the result is, things are working out. The only thing I lack is some letters from you, as I haven't received any here yet. I hope you will write soon. We've had snow and it's bitterly cold: what a contrast with Salonika!

I leave you with a hug.

Your big son,

Pierre

21 December 1917

Dear Little Mum,

At last, a letter from you! I was particularly glad because it suggested that you still have confidence in your big lad.

Apart from that, Mum, I think we are on the same wavelength – the first letter I sent you from here expresses just the attitude that you hope I have.

My letter was a bit too negative considering my new life here. I'm getting used to it and getting stuck into the work. It's better now that I feel generally more at ease. I am calmer and more mature, though still young, and this enables me to deal with things better than some of the older men here. My life as a rake is finished, trust me. I have recognised how empty and vain it is.

What a very important thing experience is: I have burned my fingers, but this has only given me pause to reflect more deeply on the right path to follow. Dear Mum, trust me. Give me another chance and you won't be disappointed.

I've done some stupid things, I admit, and I ask you to forgive me. To be really happy I would like to get a long letter from you which showed me that you can wipe out the past. I've been stupid with money, too, but that's all past now: if I ask you for money now it will be because I really need it.

A big kiss on your neck, Mum, so that you'll forgive me.

Pierre

27 December 1917

Dear Little Mum,

A couple of words to excuse myself for not having written: we are near Rupt-sur-Moselle to see demonstrations of cars and lorries. Tomorrow we're going back to base, so I hope to find lots of letters from you there.

It's damned cold here: minus 15°C.

RUPT-sur-MOSELLE (Vosges). - Vue générale, prise de l'Est

Rupt-sur-Moselle, 1917. (Private collection)

Your young gentleman, still purposeful and brave,
Pierre

28 December 1917
Dear Little Popo,

Here's a picture of the glorious scenery where I'm going to be living for a month. The mountains and the valley are a foot and a half deep in snow. It's wonderful, if rather cold!

Big hugs to you and everyone at home.
Pierre

From Rupt-sur-Moselle, two postcards bearing the same date:

3 January 1918
Dear Little Popo,

What's this? Christmas and the New Year gone by without a single letter from you? Have you forgotten me? OK, it's fine for you to study, but what about your big brother? Come on, be nice, or I'll get mad and never write to you again.

Big hugs,
Pierre

3 January 1918
Dear Little Mum,

Could you please find a book shop and order Lieutenant De Montgrand's book called *Automobiles, Camions et Tracteurs*[7] for me, and send it here as quickly as you can.

Could you also send my algebra book with the brown cover – it's with my old books.

Big hugs,
Pierre

15 January 1918
Dear Little Mum,

A little bit of chat: first of all to tell you that the parcel which I so much wanted has now arrived. Thanks Mum, for the bag and the puttees[8] and all that. Can there be another such mother on the surface of the earth? You didn't send the underpants, but it doesn't matter because I've still got the other pair. I could, though, do with another Rasurel jumper, as I've been wearing this one since I left Montauban! So that means I'm just waiting for the two books, the waterproof rubber cape and the jumper.

Nothing much else to say, except that I'm working well. I enjoy learning new things each day. I don't think it's realistic to think of becoming a Second Lieutenant because it is well established that you have to be aged 25, and anyway I couldn't care less. So long as I make it to corporal or sergeant I shall have a more comfortable existence in a small unit where I can get back to my studies for (*veterinary*) college.

Now that I have started work again I think my increased confidence will enable me to carry it through successfully. I'm not joking, Mum, this is the truth!

It's still bitterly cold. Where there was a foot and a half of snow there is now more than three feet of it. God, when will it end?

Never mind, let's be patient. The end of the war is approaching faster than most people think.

Goodbye for now and big hugs,
Pierre

19 January 1918
Dear Grandpa,

At last a moment of peace to write and thank you for your kind letter and the money order with it. Thank you both for keeping up with the Christmas traditions even though far away. It seems an age since we used to spend Christmas so happily in the family circle. Those occasions used to give us so much joy, and I really think the pleasure they give us to be among the deepest and long-lasting in our lives. Without that, lost in the snow of the Vosges, I can only be with you in spirit. Perhaps those pleasures can even be magnified by having to be contemplated from far away? Separated from all physical contact, my heart feels even closer to yours; thus, thinking of things which are no more, little Pierre realises how much he ought to love and cherish you.

Thank you particularly, Grandpa, for the forgiveness you have shown me. I am full of remorse, and very happy to see that you have a big enough heart to overlook what has gone on. Yes, I shall keep on the right road, with only the slightest unavoidable deviations. I hope that I shall succeed without too much difficulty, and get into a position where I can pay you back for your tremendous efforts on our behalf.

---

7   *Cars, Lorries and Tractors.* [T's N]
8   Woolen leg wraps worn by all armies of the period. [T's N]

As far as a career as a vet is concerned, I've hinted at the way I see it. Any occupation can be of interest if you throw yourself into it heart and soul.

With that, everything falls into place: I shall be a vet; I shall get married; I shall have a little wife and (no doubt) some youngsters whom I shall love. Over that time I shall have matured, and have had plenty of time to rid myself of illusions, and so in the end "all will be for the best in the best of all possible worlds"[9].

I leave you now, Grandpa, with big hugs.

P. Suberviolle (*rather than his usual 'Pierre'*)

23 January 1918

Dear Little Mum,

Eight days to go and the course is finished. I had the third interview today and it went off really well as usual. It looks as if I shall be able to deal with anything they throw at me, but what will your string pulling[10] bring forth? In a week we shall know.

Could you please, Mum, send me the waterproof? The snow has changed to rain now. Basically I would rather be in Salonika!

Speaking of Salonika, I can still feel the effects of being too much in the damned sun there. Sometimes when I am working on something electrical I suddenly find I can't see anything. I've tried some of the other fellows' glasses and I'm fearful of losing my ability to see close-up objects. As soon as the course has finished I shall go to an optician. It's some consolation that I shall only have to wear them for work. Do you think this is just fatigue? I'm afraid that it has been caused by the heat of the sun in Salonika which has in some way burned my eyes.

I've written by the same post to Aunt Marguerite to thank her for the socks. Now I've got everything I need.

Considering the amount of time the post is taking, could you send me the February money-order? After the course has finished I shall be off who knows where, and that will entail all the business of change of address and longer delays. It would be helpful if I had the money before that, so that I don't find myself stuck without any.

I'm still waiting for the vehicle book, and I fear it will arrive after I've taken the exam. It's no great problem as it will always be useful. I have to go now as the course is starting.

Big hugs,

Pierre

29 January 1918

Dear Mum,

I'm quite happy. We are here at Ramonchamp where we have just taken our first examination. The first paper was on 'Command and military training' and it went really well, Mum. I didn't think I was strong enough to command a whole troop, but you know I always take the lead.

After that two more papers, one maths and the other technical, and then it's all

---

9   The quote is from Voltaire's *Candide* (1759) in which the author spoke tongue in cheek, as presumably Pierre also does here. [T's N]

10   The French term for "pulling strings" is *pistonner*. Pierre, having been sent to a motor transport unit instead of the infantry in 1914, appears to have benefitted from this already. [T's N]

over. No problem with these two, and I think I shall come top, or certainly in the top three.

The smart yellow shoes, the gaiters and a fancy cap have given me the air of a top-class officer in spite of my normal ordinary suit. A bit of style and a face that's not too ugly are the important things (you didn't design me too badly, Mum!)

I'm not quite sure what I'm babbling on about, because I'm so chuffed with this morning's effort on the part of the course which had given me the most trouble. I'm quite thrilled.

This morning we had the visit from Commandant Arboux, who chatted with our CO before inspecting us. When he saw me I saw a small smile of satisfaction on his face. Have you spoken to him? What did you say to him[11]? Write quickly, because in a week I shall make a decision.

I must stop now. Big hugs,

Pierre

P.S. Did you send me the February money? I really need it before I leave here.

31 January 1918

Dear Little Mum,

I'm quickly on to the task of replying to your nice long letter which has just arrived. I'm going to go through it carefully before answering all your questions.

First of all thank you for the money. Three days ago I sent you a card telling you that I'd got it. Don't worry, Mum, I'm still determined to stick to what I've decided to do. I'm also going to send Grandpa a long letter.

First, as to the Commandant. As soon as I got here I wrote to him as agreed. He at once telephoned through to have me put on the officer training course, and that's that. Keep in with Mrs Arboux[12] without overdoing it, and we'll soon see where we get, because Fernand Darné was right. When you "pull strings", it has to be with someone really important.

The young fellows here with me are basically nonentities, but they are all from influential families with all the clout you could wish for. It's a remarkable thing that on the course we just did, it was influence which decided the outcome rather than the worth of the individual.

Apart from that I have just heard something that really worried me. After the course, if we want to continue with the officer training we have to sign up for five years! FIVE YEARS??? That could be a very bad move! The war will be over in three months and I've got to get straight off to college so that I can take some of the load off Grandpa!

As a result I am throwing myself into the work, firstly because I'm interested in cars and secondly to get to be a corporal and so have an easy time. Am I not right to do this?

Trust your son, Mum. He has sworn to be reasonable, and he is being reasonable, and he will continue to be reasonable! On top of that he is very happy because you have forgiven him all his little mistakes.

---

11   Pierre's mother had cultivated a friendship with this senior officer and expects a pay-off on her son's behalf. [T's N]

12   With the hope that this relationship will produce favourable results. [T's N]

You asked me about the place we're in. It's Rupt-sur-Moselle, a little place with twenty or so houses and two large factories, all of which are thickly covered with snow. All around there are mountains on which the pinewoods form dark patches which relieve the monotonous whiteness of the rest. One might almost say that the Good Lord had wrapped up the land in white paper to send it to another world! Here in a few words is a description of the place where I am going to live for one more month.

You spoke about Christmas. I found it a sad time. The only significant comfort I took from it was going to midnight Mass. It was odd to see the winding line of lanterns snaking its way towards the church along the path in the snow. In the church, too, I was sad, and I was filled with emotion at being so alone and far from you, Popo, Granny and Grandpa. I may even have had a tear in the corner of my eye. Let's not go on about that, because it upsets me.

Instead let's talk about the New Year, for which I send you all my best wishes. I hope I can sum them up briefly by saying first that I hope you will all be well, and then may your good young man soon be home, and all your hopes realised.

Big hugs,
Pierre

6 February 1918

Dear Mum,

At last the training course is finished, and I'm happy to tell you that I came first out of the 26 candidates, among them a sergeant and six corporals. I have straight away been awarded my corporal's stripes. I hope you will be pleased, Mum, at this evidence that when your young man sets his mind to something, he pretty easily manages it.

Commandant Arboux sent his congratulations, saying how happy he was at my success. This evening I've nothing much to do, so I'll tell you all about our conversation, because there's something I have to take up with you (but not too severely).

I now know my posting. I'm going to join the assault artillery, but don't upset yourself, as I have to get there first and the training will take ages.

I sent you a telegram this morning asking you to hurry and send my February money. It's ten days since I asked you for it, and the situation I foresaw is indeed coming to be. There are all sorts of arrangements to be made before I leave here.

More tonight.
Big hugs,
Pierre

This is the first letter in which Pierre mentions "Assault Artillery". This was in fact the French Tank Corps, of which little at that time was known. The British, having introduced tanks for the first time on the Somme in September 1916, were followed by the French during the disastrous Nivelle Offensive in April 1917 with mixed results. Since then, their overall potential clearly recognised, the tank service had expanded exponentially.

7 February 1918

Dear Little Mum,

I hope you are happy with me at last! You see that when I want something I get it! Grandfather, too, should be delighted, as I am, at my promotion to corporal. No

Pierre with a tank in battle-damaged condition. (Private collection)

more fatigues!

But Mum, why did you have to tell the Commandant that I spent my leave running wild and spending money like water? He very kindly told the whole story in front of all the others, and I was so angry that I was on the point of telling him to mind his own business! I am not in favour of public castigation like this.

He then turned to praising me, and asked me some searching questions on the blackboard. I gave good answers, and he was very pleased, though also quite surprised, given what you'd said to him about me being a drunken layabout![13]

In passing this exam, which covered a lot of detail in a short time, I have given proof, Mum, of my ability to achieve a goal when I have set my mind to it. When I have made a promise, I keep it.

As to what lies in store for me, no need for you to worry. We're going to man the tanks, so let's accept that cheerfully, and everything will come out right as it always has. Deep down I'm quite happy with this outcome. Considering my class[14] it could well have been the infantry for me. I am still undecided, though, as to whether I should make an application to be an airman.

Now that I've got a bit more spare time I shall be able to write to you more often and at greater length.

Big hugs,

Pierre

P.S. If you write to the Barthes, could you mention my success in the exam and

---

13   Demonstrating that the commandant knew perfectly well that strings were being pulled and was happy, though somewhat surprised, to find among all the "nonentities ... from influential families" (Pierre's words) he had promoted someone worthwhile. [T's N]

14   Pierre's phrase "considering my class" refers to his age group. All young men were statistically categorised by their year of birth. Thus government authorities subsequently utilised these figures to determine how many from each class would be available for military service. [T's N]

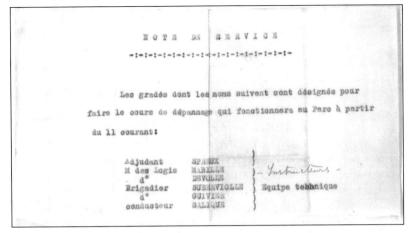

Order assigning Pierre to a tank maintenance course as instructor. (Private collection)

that I'm going into tanks? This will prepare the ground in case I am sent near Paris for my tank training, in which case I can go and see them!!!! Don't laugh, Mum.

13 February 1918
Dear Little Mum,

I'm sending you this to prove to you that I wasn't just boasting: I was a pupil, and here I am a teacher!

I'm in the next draft for the tanks, but don't worry yourself. As soon as I get settled in the new posting I shall use my success in the exam to get myself on to an artillery officer training course. There isn't an age limit for that, like there is for transport officers.

It's some time since I heard anything from you or Popo. Is everything all right?

Have you sent the money? I am anxious to have it because it is nearly time for me to make the move. I hope Grandpa will be proud enough of his grandson to add a little something to my allowance! I've earned it!

So you see, Mum, that when your big lad sets his mind to something, he manages it. You can be sure that will be the case *throughout his life*.

Big kisses,
Pierre

8

Teaching theories to idiots who understand nothing

Pierre was transferred from the Vosges front to Fleury-les-Aubrais armour training centre near Orleans in mid-February 1918. Here he was taught how to drive tanks in order to instruct others as the war continued. The United States had entered the War the previous April; this was followed by an influx of American troops on French soil. This timely arrival subsequently offset the initial gains made during a series of great German spring offensives designed to bring France and Great Britain to terms before American manpower made a significant impact. On 27 May the Germans began a new offensive on the Aisne. Paris was threatened; it was not until 15 July that this push was halted on the Marne. The spring offensives cost the Germans a million casualties, of which 300,000 were killed. On 18 July a Franco-American counter-attack began, in which tanks played a decisive part.

22 February 1918

Dear Little Mum,

I've been in this training camp for four days, and already I am an ace in the true sense of the word. Our team of corporals has won the prize for the best result. To win we had to drive our four tanks as fast as we could over trenches and deep ditches. It was great, and I am very excited.

With a few more days' instruction I shall graduate from being a pupil to being a teacher, and so I shan't be moving on from here. I hope that this in turn will give me the chance to get into artillery officer training. There is no age limit for that, and I can say goodbye to the transport branch. I shan't be a column dodger any more, and ahead lies glory!

For the moment, as I said, we are in the depths of a forest, to maintain maximum secrecy. It's life in the rough again, like in Salonika. We have nowhere to go to eat out, but at least our basic rations are reasonable.

Could you please, Mum, as quickly as you can, send me: some big size smart writing paper; my Meerschaum pipe in the form of a 'death's head' with my initials in black on it; sheepskin gloves with no fur on the outside (which I need to operate the tank controls better); and some *tobacco*. I'd like you to send me tobacco regularly, please, as there is nowhere here I can buy any. One advantage of being out here is that at least I can't get into my normal line of mischief!

I'm impatient for news. I don't know what to make of the situation in which you find yourself. Don't worry, and above all look after yourself. Everything sorts itself out in life, and you just need to be prepared to wait while it does.

That's all now, so big hugs,

Pierre

Pierre (top right) during tank training. (Private collection)

28 February 1918

Little Mum,

I'm in haste to tell you about my first day in the new branch of the service. I've begun my training and am completely bowled over. These little machines are wonderful, well protected, reliable and they go anywhere. I can't say any more.

Don't upset yourself, Mum, because I'm likely to be here for ages. Almost all my old mates from Salonika are here, goodness knows how, but I was fated to come here …

13 March 1918

Little Mum,

I'm glad I didn't write back immediately on receiving your long letter in which I thought you were unfair.

Since my time at Rupt, I had thought that all these old stories had been buried. Since I promised you (that I would reform) have I not kept my promise? I came out top at Rupt, earned my corporal's stripes, got put straight in to the tanks and qualified as an instructor in six days. My reports are good and it's on the cards that I shall soon be made up to warrant-officer[1]. I'm still also hoping to be sent to Fontainebleau[2]. Haven't I given enough proof of my good intentions?

Anyway, once and for all, let's forget the past. I hug you tight.

As far as women are concerned I hope you will accept that I have ceased to have anything to do with them and I don't write to them. Please calm down, and *don't be jealous*! Come on, Mum, smile and be nice to your big lad. You know this scallywag loves you more than anyone else!

---

1   *Sous-officier*: Non-commissioned rank equivalent to a Sergeant-Major. [T's N]
2   Presumably for artillery officer training. [T's N]

St Ètienne Mle 1907 Machine-gun c. 1914. (Private collection)

You can see that everything is going well at the moment. I have been a bit tired, probably because the physical effort needed to do the training at Rupt was beyond anything I was used to. I've also got a touch of malaria which slows me down a bit. Working out in the open air in the great forest has quickly put me right.

I can tell you that I'm back to working like a nigger[3] again. I have to do algebra, geography and history, all of which I shall need if I go to Fontainebleau. I'm even stuffing myself with History, if you can believe it, eh, Mum?

A bit about where I am in my life. Our lair lies deep in the forest, far from any dwelling places. The tanks, manoeuvrable little steel boxes, are on the move everywhere you look. Inside them it's very hot, and you only have a few little holes to see where you're going. I hope this simple description will pass the censor! The machine guns are also pretty handy. They hit hard and are good to handle, especially against the Boches. In brief I think I shall have a fine time in these devilish little machines.

You should be able to tell from these few details that there is nothing very alarming here that you need to upset yourself about. The worst thing about the place is the daily routine, which goes as follows:

- Reveille at 6.00 a.m.
- Military training
- Driving ordinary vehicles (I teach that)
- Vehicle maintenance (I teach that, too)

In the late afternoon we have:

- Driving tanks (I teach that)
- Use of the machine gun
- Cleaning the tanks

That's not all, because at 6.00 p.m., after our meal, (and also at breakfast time) we have to do all the chores involved in running the camp, of which, by God, there are a lot.

You can see from this, Mum, that I'm fully occupied all day, and many evenings

---

3   Appropriate language for a man of his time, when the vast majority of Europeans held racist views.[T's N]

I'm too exhausted to write. You have written to me so often recently that I want to pay you back in kind. However smelly I get, I shall only wash myself up once every two days, to make time to write to you a lot! I expect you to be equally assiduous, OK?

Back to my life here. The worst thing is guard duty. In the artillery it isn't like being in transport: I've got thirty blokes under me, several of them pretty rough diamonds and all of them older than me. What can the young corporal do to one of these bad lots to make him do what he's told? I get there in the end but not without a bit of shouting, I can tell you. I don't punish them, but I've become skilled in the art of bawling at them.

There you are, Mum, a few glimpses of my life. Does that reassure you? As to wandering off the strait and narrow, forget it. The only time I get off camp is to go every Sunday with Durand to a little village three miles away to get our laundry done. We then avail ourselves of a devilish good little restaurant in a lodging house there, where we treat ourselves to a whopping big dinner, which we've earned. One feast a week is not overdoing it, I think.

Do you like this kind of chatter? I really look forward to your next letter, you naughty Mummy! Remember that your letters are about the only thing that's good about life here. I am helped by being relieved that Grandpa is feeling better. (Tell, him, by the way, not to blab too much to Mr. Fénié. I've written to him and it will all work out given time.)

Now then, Mum, the clouds have rolled away and the sun is shining again. Wasn't I right to say 'Don't upset yourself'? I thought that our difficulty was going to be worse than it was. Everything is back to normal, so let's see a smile back on your lips again.

So, Mum, your big tank man jumps up to kiss your neck and give you a big hug.

Pierre

P.S. You know, you can be proud of your son, now that he is not just a common or garden driver. My stripes are red rather than green, and I wear a little black beret rather than the kepi of a column-dodger. On my chest sparkles the tank badge, almost as prestigious as a pilot's.

To set against Pierre's boyish enthusiasm for his new toy, the tank, here are a few lines from Erich Maria Remarque's *All Quiet on the Western Front*, which depicts tanks from the infantryman's point of view:

> The tanks, once a joke, have now become fearful. In their long armoured columns they epitomize for us more than anything else the horror of war ... The lines of enemy attackers are composed of human beings like ourselves, but these tanks are just machines, with their tracks moving remorselessly on, like the war itself. They bring destruction as, emotionless, they plunge into craters and emerge again without any interruption of their progress. The great armoured fleet thunders forward, belching smoke. The steel beasts crush beneath them the wounded and the dead.

18 March 1918 (*to his sister*)

Oh Mimi,

It's hard to keep my mind on the same subject for two minutes. A bloke who has been doing acrobatics is now playing the accordion while two soldiers are dancing. It's

Tank column at the halt. Photo by Pierre Suberviolle. (Private collection)

pandemonium in here: there are two smoky lamps and the air is full of tobacco smoke. You can see how easy it is to write peacefully ...

20 March 1918

Dear Little Mum,

Don't be jealous just because my last few letters were all addressed to Popo! She is really charming, my little sister, and you have no idea how much good her letters do me. They help me to feel that I am more fully a part of your lives. I like her friendly chatter which gives away how much she loves her big brother. Then there are the little sketches and a thousand other little touches which show how hard she is trying to please me. In this lonely rat-hole it is really charming to read them.

23 March 1918

Little Mum,

Guess where I'm writing this! In the sick-bay! I've got pimples growing on me like branches on a tree, and I suspect my hands are about to burst into flower. I've got scabies.

It was inevitable. I've had so many different billets and been in contact with so many men in various states of cleanliness, and with so many changes of blankets, and with there being an epidemic of it, here in camp I've caught it like many others have.

I came in here this morning and I don't yet know what treatment they are going to put me on. Don't worry about me. I'm being well fed and pretty well accommodated in the little wards. I think I'll be all right for the time it takes to put me right.

25 March 1918

Little Mum,

What a lovely sunny day! I'm truly beginning to love France! I'm in the middle of the park, spread out on a lounger, and able to admire nature to my heart's content. It's true that my skin is burning, and indeed, by God, this morning was terrible with the second shower and the second treatment with the ointment. I scrub myself with the brush as much as I can, and I feel the improvement already. In two or three days I shall be fine again, and I look forward to it impatiently even though it isn't really all that long to wait.

Crossing off the days on my calendar, I notice that yesterday was Palm Sunday. How quickly the time passes and how many happy memories I have of that day!

Do you remember how much we looked forward to that lovely and blessed day when I was young? First because it was the first day of the holidays, and then there was the little celebration of preparing the olive branches and stealing some of Grandma's sweets. Then we went off to Mass with me happily holding the heavy load in my little hand. At last we got back home and quickly ate our dessert, and then I was let loose on the thousand goodies hanging in the olive tree branches.

What a long time ago that was! And what a very private pleasure in remembering it! The present time is hard to endure, as the war goes on for ever. When we are old, I think there will be a certain pleasure in remembering this time of pain and suffering[4]. The war can't last long now, and we can only hope that we get through it alive.

At the moment things are moving quickly, not altogether how you'd like, but I feel that the end is approaching. They are still shelling Paris, and this will go on.

I've not had any letters since I came in here, so I hope I will have some soon.

Big kisses,

Pierre

At the beginning of April we discover the location of Pierre's "lair". It was at Cercottes in the Loiret, an enormous camp for reservists and recruit training.[5] As Pierre relates the following May:

... the days are getting more beautiful, but God, how hot it is! I'm worried it's going to get worse than Salonika was! In all this great camp, surrounded by woodland, there is hardly a breath of air, or the slightest breeze to cool our boiling brains! On top of that the marshlands are drying out, and as a result there are clouds of mosquitoes everywhere. These are the joys of Cercottes Camp.

Pierre's worries were financial and romantic respectively, as the following letters attest:

15 April 1918

Little Mum,

I am asking you for some money: here is a list of the things I had to buy:

Train fare 11.50	Repaying debts 40.00
Mess Bill 10.00	Jacket 50.00
Trousers 50.00	History Book 6.00
Geography Book 4.00	Geometry Book 4.00
Spacial Geometry 4.00	Exercise Book 2.00
Gloves 10.00	Sulphur bath 15.00
Oil Lamp 5.00	Beret 9.00
	TOTAL 200.00 F

---

4   Pierre, perhaps unwittingly, reached the same conclusion as Virgil (70-19 BC) two millennia earlier when the latter credited Aeneas with the ironic phrase *Forsan et haec olim meminisse iuvabit* – "Someday it will be a pleasure to remember even these sufferings." [T's N]

5   Cercottes was the first training facility that AS personnel went to before finishing their training at the main *AS* base at Champlieu. The site was chosen because it was close to the main *DSA* base at Orléans and was managed by the DSA, something that caused much friction with the *AS*.

Cercottes Camp, 1918. (Private collection)

The shirt and trousers were the most expensive but I had to have them to cut a dash in Fontainebleau. For this I dipped into my reserve which I had done well to ask you for in advance. In four or five days we're off again, but I don't know where. I would like you to send me 100 francs for that, Mum. Just put a banknote in a registered letter and send it to Mr. Boisvieux. He will send it on to me. The army won't bother to find me!

I'm looking forward to getting a bit nearer the front, because if we stay in this God-forsaken place, we'll be bored to death. I hope that my wish will soon be granted, and that soon they will come through ...

I still haven't got a proper military address, so go on writing to the same address.

Big hugs.

Pierre

Tuesday 15 April 1918

Little Mum,

I've just visited Saint-Géniès[6], which was a painful experience. He told me, Mother, that you were unhappy and furious with me. OK, you can be 'furious': but, Mother, what I forbid you to say, (it's not an order, but a prayer) never say that I don't love you, never!

You know that it is for you alone, and for little Popo that up to now I have been determined to save my skin. If it were not for you, dear beloved Mum, and my little sister, I would have given up on the world a long time ago, and would be dead by now.

Mum, I'm suffering, and even tearful, but I don't say that I don't love you. How dare you say such a thing?

I say no more, but I kiss you on your neck and on your eyes, because, dear Mum, you have just done me great harm. I ask that you leave me to cry awhile with my head on your shoulder.

I'm only speaking of things which weigh heavily on my heart at the moment, Mum. About everything else I say nothing. On Sunday, *come what may*, I shall come to Montauban.

Mother, write to me but don't nag me anymore. At this moment I am depressed and capable of anything.

---

6   This mysterious individual makes several fleeting appearances in Pierre's correspondence, but sadly his identity cannot be determined. [T's N]

Renault FT17 Tank images from Pierre's album. (Private collection)

If you wish it, dear Mum, I give you a kiss and a hug.
P. Suberviolle

19 April 1918 (*hastily scribbled in pencil*)
Little Mum,

I've had bad luck. This morning when I got back from teaching I found my jacket in the billet but my wallet wasn't in it. What really made me mad was that I had just received your registered letter.

You can see, Mother, the difficulty I'm in, so please send me something quickly, still c/o Mr. Boisvieux. I've got to rush for the roll-call.

Big hugs,
Pierre

Wednesday 24 April 1918
Dear Grandpa,

A word in your ear, because I need your help. Mum is so good that I don't want to worry her. As I'm sure you know from the note I sent her, I've had my wallet pinched with more than 150 francs in it. I've just this minute got the letter from Popo with the thirty francs in it. I need some cash to repay what the other lads have lent me.

So, Grandpa, this time it's you I'm asking. You are well aware of the role which tanks play in battle, and the many risks we run of getting hit. I therefore ask you, Grandpa, to send me 200 francs, 100 to tuck away at the bottom of my wallet, and 100 to have some fun before I go up into the line. Could you do that very quickly, as on Monday or Tuesday we are moving?

Could you send the money to Mr. Boisvieux at Fleury-les-Aubrais from Tuesday 30th.

You can write to me at:

P. Suberviolle, Brigadier Instructeur[7] H.D. 8 – P.A.O.C. Camp des Cercottes – par les Aydes (Loiret)

Grandpa, that's all for now. Thanks in anticipation and with big hugs, and then I'm off to roll-call

Big hugs,
Pierre

Pierre ended his letter of 2 May by stating: "With or without leave I'm coming to give you a hug on Sunday". On 7 May he mentions the trip went well, and that Mr Barthe had been a charming companion. Thus he managed to get away and go to Montauban.

10 May 1918
I need to have a chat with you, little Mum. I am very depressed in this great camp at Cercottes. Today the weather is terrible, with freezing fog piercing us to the marrow. It feels as if the light has been strained through the blanket of fog and can hardly reach us. On the ground there is mud and water – it's a real bog.

Lots of fun running in front of tanks all day or teaching theories to people who

---

7   A French brigadier is a cavalry corporal; a British Brigadier is of general officer's rank.

haven't got a clue about them. But it's that or something worse ...

A little tale: I've just inflicted my first punishment! There was this guy who was older than me, wouldn't listen to what I was saying and finally gave me cheek. I was pretty annoyed because I generally treat them well, so I gave him two days jankers[8], and the lieutenant upped it to four. See how fierce I've become? Discipline, ah! Discipline above everything!

These are the sort of little things that happen and help to pass the time, and trust me, it needs help passing!

Tomorrow the training comes to an end and I shall no doubt find out what is in store for me.

If I'm free tomorrow, might I make it down to Montauban? Maybe, and if I do I'll give you a big hug.

Big kisses,

Pierre

The following letter states Pierre had returned to Montauban. Twice in a fortnight? Surprising to say the least.

14 May 1918

My dear Little Mum,

Yesterday I only had time to send a quick word to Popo to put you at rest about the journey.

Oh, Mum! Didn't I do well to come? This week has flashed by without moping or negative thoughts. And why was that? Because my heart was full of your and Popo's love.

This is the way it is with men, Mum. I fear that 'Out of sight, out of mind' has a certain amount of truth in it. There's never really forgetting, of course, because thanks to the lovely letters I get from both of you, my heart is always yours. Even so, without the little touches and signs of affection, and family chitchat, things do become more distant.

It's just at such a moment that someone passes, perhaps a woman who notices you, and straight away your heart goes out to her, happy to find some sign of affection. Too easily you become as if drunk with happiness, and it's then that the silly things start to happen ...

That is the mental state of any soldier who serves too long without home leave.

Everything indeed in this monotonous, rigid and insipid military life impels man towards a life with more love in it where he has at least the illusion of no longer living like a beast.

This is one of the laws of war. Have not love affairs always been entangled with combat? In Antiquity love and war were inextricably linked[9], and our medieval knights constructed the edifice of courtly love in which it was noble to be killed for love of a woman. More recently didn't Napoleon's wars give the French the reputation of being chivalrous?

---

8   Army term for a period of punishment. See <http://uk.answers.yahoo.com/question/index?qid=20061227095710AA9WAzQ> [T's N]

9   He might well have mentioned the Trojan War [T's N]

I finish my little lecture with some random words which are nevertheless apposite:

war – soldiers: love, wine and tobacco.

What do you think of this, Mum. I shall look forward to your reply with interest!
Big kisses,
Pierre

16 May 1918

Little Mum,

I am in a devilish bad mood. I've got to stay attached to the 12th battalion as an instructor. I've been to see the captain and the camp commandant, but they say I'm too good an instructor to be let go. Result, four more weeks in Cercottes and I can do nothing about it.

I would have been very happy to go to the front. I'd have spent two or three months in the woods at Champlieu, and then we'd have gone into the line. Maybe it's lucky for me. Perhaps I might have been killed? We need to be fatalistic and see what destiny brings.

I'm writing to you from Orleans, Mum, but don't worry yourself about that because I am always in control of myself. Mind you, that's not without effort and a test of my character! Listen, little Mum, I'm going to tell you a few secrets:

Since my return from Montauban I have been at peace, and I've got back to my studies to finish my course. This evening, furious at the news that I am to be kept here, I went back to Orleans to blot out the memory. But guess who I met there in the street? First we just held hands like old friends, and then we began to chat, and soon there was a tear in her eye; she was sorry, she pleaded and she begged, but Mum, I stayed strong.

Leaving her a few moments later I didn't know what to do with myself. I was pulled this way and that by thinking first of you, and the promise I made to you, and then of her lovely eyes full of tears; I was in turmoil, real turmoil, and it was only by thinking of you that I managed to stop myself running after her. I was pleased that I managed to resist the temptation, Mum, but it cost me a lot to do it. I still feel bad, but at the same time I am glad to suffer for the sacrifice I made.

And why was this, Mum? Because you are so, so good to me, and I take account of how much you love me and your generosity towards me; you have found the right way to make Pierre respect your views.

What are you going to make of this letter? I'm chatting here to my big sister, and telling her my problems. I know my big sister will understand, and so my heart is on the mend already.

Little Mum, lots of big hugs,
Pierre

P.S. Dear Mum, I would like to take advantage of the few days left to me before my next course starts to come down to Montauban again. Could you send a telegram saying that you or Popo are ill, and I am urgently needed at home? The sooner you do this the better, then if I don't get leave they might make an exception for me. Send it to Suberviolle, Brigadier H.D.8 – 500th Regiment of Artillery [sic][10], Cercottes Camp, par les Aydes (Loiret).

---

10   500th Régiment Artillerie Spéciale. This was the depot regiment for the entire *AS*.

17 May 1918

Little Mum,

What a lovely day we've just had: everything is coming to life again in the May sun, which is already quite hot!

This evening, while I was making my way from camp over to Fleury, over the backroads and along the footpaths, I could smell, almost taste Nature renewing itself. The new grass is very green and packs itself tightly together as if it wanted to cover all the land. And then, as if embarrassed by the uniform greenness, it allows space for the buttercups and daisies, which it sets off like a picture frame.

The bushes and trees are in leaf, and seem in a hurry to fill themselves up with colourful twittering bird-life. Sparrows and finches chase each other madly round the branches which yesterday were bare and today are unrecognisable.

Everything full of light and life with the colours made more vivid by the light of the setting sun. Everything is smiling and happy. What do you care, Mother Nature, about the adventures and follies of us humans? We, like them, are just little insects which rush about your world. Here's a May Bug being chased along the road by two golden beetles; I don't give tuppence for them, and give them the merest glance before going on my way. That's just the way you treat us. What do you care if a man suffers or dies? Maybe you're right, because compared with you man is nothing much.

And yet man is something, and sometimes something great. He has a great soul, and this soul thinks, reflects, and can suffer. I'm speaking for myself, Mum, but I find that between the massive calm of Nature and my inner turmoil there is too great a gulf for comfort. Why is life like this? Why shouldn't we, too, have our future path marked out, free of worries and cares? Adam certainly blundered when he shared the apple with Eve: had he not done so, wouldn't we have been happy until the end of time?

Got to go now, so big hugs,

Pierre

He then has a period of leave at home; evidently the telegram (see the postscript to his letter of 16 May) had borne fruit!

28 May 1918

Dear Little Mum,

I'm really down again, so time to chat with you. It's pretty dreadful after a nice visit at home to be stuck back in the mind-numbing routine in this camp.

I must admit, though, that I've got a very cushy situation: I spend my morning preparing my lectures and making some diagrams for the other instructors to use. In the afternoon, between 1.00 and 3.00 I lecture 150 blokes without stopping. You should know that the two lieutenants never miss a session. They are charming and think highly of me. I'm pretty glad about that, because I'll shortly be leaving with them: yes, Mum, it's now official that when the course has finished, I'm going to be sent to join the 12th battalion.

I'm looking forward to that, because I've had enough of Orleans, and the sooner I get out of here the better. I have had more emotional anguish since I came back here. I'll tell you about it one day but I'm not in the mood for it now. Big sister, it's really nothing, and the regrets fade away with time.

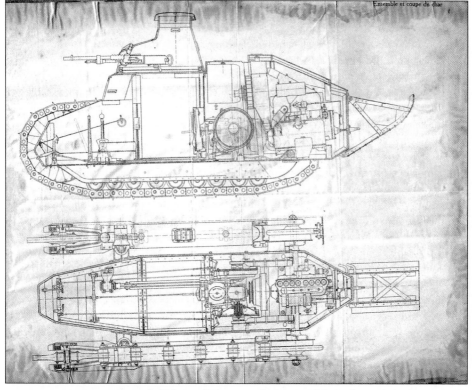

Renault FT17 tank diagram. (Private collection)

Anyway, Mum, here I am with my feet on the ground again and happier because of it (assuming that you write to me often).

Big hugs,

Pierre

31 May 1918

Little Mum,

I really loved your last letter, which lifted my spirits. I have been troubled, believe it, but I have been strong enough to get through it and continue to deserve your love. Listen, Big Sister: little Pierre's heart was wounded, but it is now healed.

Yes Mum, that girl had her claws into me, and I'll tell you how I found a radical cure. I had the misfortune to bump into her again after I came back off leave, and she was more beautiful than ever.

Resistance was useless, and I went back to her house. That was last Monday.

Then money came up. I couldn't oblige her, as I only had 50 francs, which I'd left in my wallet with my pal Crinon. I'd told him on no account to give me any of it!

Result, on Wednesday night everything went wrong, and by Thursday, our affair came to an abrupt end!

So that was all right, there was something else to complete the healing process. When I tore myself away from her on Thursday morning I thought she loved me, but what do I see on Thursday evening? There she is on the arm of an officer!

Allow me to inform you, dear Mum, that your son is the *King of Fools*!

In life one only learns by experience. I hope that this particular lesson will serve me well and enable me to cope with the future more successfully!

What can you be thinking, Little Mum, of this confession? Your big lad has been open with you and you can be sure that in this contest between his love for a strange woman and his love for his mother, it's his love for his mother which has come out on top. Only your love is deep enough to sustain your big lad's courage.

I look forward eagerly to a long letter from you.

Very big kisses,

Pierre

3 June 1918

Little Mum,

This evening I went for a walk into Orleans, mostly to get out of this dump, as I've had enough of it.

I'm not fed up with the job, and in fact I'm getting a taste for it because it gets me known among the officers. Every morning I prepare my talk, and I do it carefully because I know that officers will be there listening to it. In the afternoon two full hours of non-stop questions and answers, which is tedious, but at least my skills as an orator are rapidly developing to the point where I can tell all my little stories without drawing breath. The rest of the afternoon is taken up by questioning the men.

You see, Mum, how busy I am, and a brief spell of duty here is fine. Even better now that I have completely recovered from the heartache, and in this respect I am particularly anxious to hear from you. Oh, yes, Little Mum, your little Pierre is still being a good boy, and the more I do it the easier it gets. Life is a question of training and habit. If you are taught to amuse yourself, you amuse yourself and get used to doing it. With a little effort one can drag oneself back to older, better ways. Which way is the better one? I think you think the second, eh, Mum? Deep down I do, too.

On another subject, you know I'm not coming home on leave? I had the papers in my hand, and then, three hours before I was due to set off, leave was cancelled. Taking it all round I'm not too upset. It hasn't been long enough since my last leave, and if I wait until I am sent into the line, I shall gain an extra three days, so in the end I'll have ten days, not seven, which is a good result.

I have to stop now, so big hugs,

Pierre

Can you send me some tobacco? I'm as miserable as sin because I haven't had a smoke in ten days!

4 June 1918

Little Mum,

I'm writing from camp, still a little shaken by a success I have had. I was giving my last lecture to the 12th battalion and I finished with something of a patriotic flourish when speaking of my high hopes for the tanks in battle. Being a bit of a tearaway it was quite an obvious line for me to take. My audience of 300 squaddies broke into loud applause in which even the officers joined.

It was not a big deal, but it pleased me all the same, considering how difficult and tiring some aspects of the technical course were, that I managed to get through without annoying my listeners too much and even teaching them a bit. The rest of the week will be taken up with testing. We are already under way with that, and some of the questions are really tough. Apart from that nothing much, Mum, and life is boring. I'm looking forward to getting a nice little tank painted yellow and green, with Nénette and Rintintin hanging one on each side of the door[11]. Then I can't come to any harm!

What's going on over there, Mum? I don't know how long it is since I had a letter from you, and Popo seems to have forgotten me as well. I have just received some pictures of me; the one where I am serious is the best. I'm a bit glum, but that's pretty normal for me these days.

Off now, so big hugs,

Pierre

P.S. Tobacco! Tobacco!

5 June 1918

I'm happy at last, because I've just got your long letter. I didn't know what you would think of me, Mum, though I guessed. I knew that you would be happy that I had broken off the relationship, and I'm very touched by something you said. You love your boy so much that you forget why he was suffering. You are so good that you're going to feel sorry for him. Thank you Mum, because hard times like those are useful in one's life. As for me, I draw several conclusions from this lesson, the first of which is not to be overconfident, and not to say 'no woman will ever get the better of me'. I must not be trusting.

Secondly, I see that true love is a rare thing, especially in casual encounters with local women who you meet when you're on the town. Unless we act without honour, relationships with such women as these require money. The pleasures of such relationships are fleeting and soon pall. They do not lead to real happiness. It is necessary and even useful for a young man to have some fun from time to time, but he mustn't go too far.

To get back to your letter. I'm pleased that Commandant Arboux made a point of telling you how much he thought of me. If I had been some kind of illiterate clumsy idiot do you think he would have said those things? Mother, his words carry weight, and you can base your opinion of me on them.

Something else. You would like me to stay at Cercottes, but that cannot be. A certain pretty little face with beautiful eyes is lurking nearby and may do harm to me whatever the strength of my resolve. That's the first thing. Next, I want to go to the front because I have confidence in the tanks. A daredevil like me is bound to achieve something. Another thing is that as soon as I leave here I shall be promoted Sergeant-Major; I'm going to feel good and I want to ride the wave. It's no more than my duty, and although my patriotism has taken some knocks there's still a bit left, especially now when things are not going well. I don't want to stay here skulking at the back, it's

---

11   *Nénette et Rintintin* were almost universally adopted as good luck talismans by the people of France during the First World War. Family and friends would reproduce these woolen homespun dolls for fathers and brothers serving with the forces. See 'Nenette and Rintintin French WW1 Mascot Postcards'<http://aboutcards.blogspot.fr/2007/07/nenette-and-rintintin-french-ww1-mascot.html> [T's N]

disgusting. I'll say a bit more tomorrow night.

Big kisses on your neck,

Pierre

Following a "secret mission" lasting some days, Pierre is in need of additional funds:

16 June 1918

Little Mum,

I sent you a quick note yesterday evening to put your mind at rest. Since then I've got more news to tell. I've been promoted to Quartermaster-Sergeant[12] in the 336th Company of the A.S. The formal announcement of my promotion will take a few days, but basically that's it. I shall be in command of two tanks, and I'm really pleased.

And what about you? I'll send you my drafting order to show it's not a wind-up. My promotion means, Mum, that I need a bit more money from you and Grandpa. I hope he will be pleased to help his young sergeant, who is looking forward to charging into battle.

The 100 francs you sent me I spent as follows:

> Room – 30 francs
> Laundry – 10 francs
> Present for Boisvieux – 20 francs
> Lent to Saint-Géniès – 20 francs (don't mention it)

That leaves 20 francs which I'm keeping for my last night out drinking in Orleans. I've got to say goodbye to the place with all its memories.

Now we're off to Gidy, 20 miles from Orleans. We'll stay there for a fortnight, and then – who knows … ?

The first time I go in the sergeants' mess it will be expected that I buy everyone a round, which will cost me at least 20 francs. My mess bill will be around 30 francs and I shall have to have my uniform jacket and trousers refitted: fifteen each makes thirty francs. There will be other bits and pieces that I need and I should think they will add up to around 120 francs. Train fares to my new posting will also cost a bit, so I reckon I need 200 francs altogether.

Because I have achieved senior NCO status, I will come out of the Fontainebleau Officer Training Course as a full lieutenant. It would be unfortunate if, for lack of funds, I could not appear properly turned out among my brother officers, especially at the first mustering of the unit[13]. I hope that you and Grandpa will understand all this and send the sum I have asked for.

Send me a money order for the 200 francs in a registered letter c/o Mr. Boisvieux. I shall send the motorbike man to pick it up on Friday; I prefer to do it this way because our military postal service is slower. Don't send any other letters apart from the money order to that address. All other letters should now be sent to

---

12   Quartermaster Sergeant: Tank Corps equivalent to sergeant of infantry. [T's N]
13   Pierre had previously mentioned thoughts of officer training, but had turned it down because of a stipulated condition of five years' subsequent military service. This he was not prepared to do because of the need to relieve his grandfather from his unexpected veterinary practice burden. [T's N]

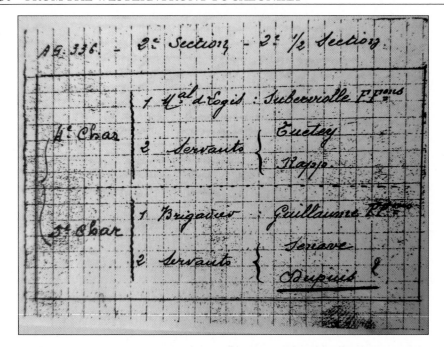

P. Suberviolle, Quartermaster-Sergeant -336th Company A.S. – Gidy – Loiret

Please Mum make haste with this, because I can't have the motorbike man go all the way over to Mr Boisvieux's place for nothing. This money is absolutely essential for my transfer to my new unit to go smoothly.

From tomorrow I shall get back into the habit of writing to you every two days.

Big kisses,

Pierre

Attached to this letter was a little piece of paper (see above), confirming Pierre's promotion in formal handwriting.

18 June 1918

Little Mum,

That's Orleans finished with, with all its delights. Here I am at Gidy, a little tiny village in the middle of the woods. Its main asset is that it is 20 miles from Orleans – I say 'asset' which is not to say that it's any fun here.

Since yesterday I've been terribly down. After the busy life I led at Orleans, I've been suddenly thrown into this complete isolation without any preparation. You've no idea how my spirit has felt crushed by the depressing effects of this change.

I could have stayed at Cercottes a bit longer, but I felt it best that I should go. For a man at the tender age of 21 there were still too many temptations. I am now a person of some standing. The officer I travelled with was charming and we travelled in comfort. I haven't yet got my stripes, but I'm there in every other sense. I eat with the officers and have the same regime as them. I can't tell you how many little perks are attached to this! Can you believe that one of them is that I have Corporal Saint-Géniès under my command! I'm quite happy to be apart from him and to keep my distance. He's nice enough, but you know what they say about him ...

Some gossip about my (brother) officers. The commandant was with the zouaves, and he has the reputation of being a tough guy. I'm glad about this. I'm sure that a little chap like me who keeps straight on and doesn't panic will be well respected.

My commanding officer in the 336th is Lieutenant Barrière, a charming man. People say he must have confidence in me, to have appointed me quartermaster. He has the great advantage of being a cavalry officer, and so a man of refinement in every detail. He will be able to rely on me, come what may.

Sub-Lieutenant Duprat[14] comes from Bordeaux. He is my immediate superior. He is also very kind. He's a sportsman and doesn't worry. He looks as if he is a graduate, so we shall get on well. Now you know all about my officers, Mum.

So what am I in the company? I'm the warrant officer in command of a half-section, with two tanks, a corporal and four soldiers. Knowing how to deal with these men I'm sure I can get them to do what I want, and that they will follow my orders without flinching. I can tell you that after I gave my talks all the fellows in the 12th battalion wanted to be with me!

What are we going to do, and what will become of us? This week we will be given our uniforms. Next week we'll get all our kit and weapons, and sometime after that we'll be off, who knows where? I'm looking forward to moving out of this jungle, as it would be just as good to be on the front line.

And Marie-Antoinette? Below is a letter from Pierre to her father:

20 June 1918
My dear Sir,

It's a long time since I gave you any indication that I was still alive. What, indeed, have I of interest to tell you now? Life at Cercottes was monotonous and without enjoyment.

Now, however, everything is changing. I am now attached to a company, that is, to a battle unit, and in a place of honour within it. I am on the point of being confirmed as a warrant officer, only lacking the badge of my rank. I have command of two tanks, one armed with an artillery piece and one with a machine gun.

I hope you feel I've done well. I have high hopes and the will to succeed. We have the shock of combat to fear, it's true, but I set out full of confidence in our little tanks.

Wouldn't you like to be with us? You would see how smart we are!

Now, my dear Sir, I have something to ask you. Now that my life is entering a more intense phase in which every moment counts double, and in which I need every ounce of determination and drive (because they call us the 'super-men'), would you allow Marie-Antoinette to be my 'godmother'?[15] The strength I shall derive from the support of my mother, Marie-Antoinette and my sister Popo will be enough to see me through the severe tests which I am about to undergo, and God knows they will be severe.

What are you going to say to this? I await your reply with impatience, and shall pay

---

14   This officer is mentioned in Appendix VI. See *Historique du 504ᵉ régiment A.S.*

15   Godmother: A woman who would regularly correspond with a soldier to boost his morale. Many of these wartime relationships ended in marriage.

careful attention to what you say.

Please accept, Dear Sir, the testimony of my most lively regard,
P. Suberviolle

We are very fortunate to have Mr. Barthe's reply to Pierre.

Brétigny, June 22nd 1918

I received your letter yesterday morning and I regret that you did not find the time to shake my hand before your departure.

Anyway I must praise the state of mind in which you are going back to war. I never doubted your energy or your courage and I congratulate you with all my heart. I do not think the war will last long now. However, there will still be heavy blows given and received. You will be among those who are giving it to the Boches; you have been lucky enough thus far, which makes us hope that you will not be one of those who get it back. It is needless to say that our concerns on your account [illegible] are serious at times and I want you to tell us your news from time to time. I come straight to the main purpose of your letter ... Before answering, I re-read the letter that you sent me in March 1917, in which your common sense and loyalty led you to recognize the force of the arguments that had impelled me to ask you not to write to Marie-Antoinette. These arguments, my poor friend, still apply and are increased by the fact that Marie-Antoinette, more sensitive and impressionable, would suffer greatly from this new situation. I want her to retain her freedom of mind and heart and I will try to keep from her anything which might upset her. There is, of course, no point in going over again the reasons why I am taking this attitude. You are sensible enough, and too good-hearted, to have forgotten them.

Write to me soon, and go on writing to me regularly. You know how I am always interested in you and all your family. I do not think you've ever doubted my affection for you and I want you to let me know how you see things. It would have been better if you had come to see me. There may still be time, so take the opportunity if you can. With affectionate good wishes,
Antonin Barthe

21 June 1918

Little Mum,

You must have laughed when you got the letter I sent to Aunt Madeleine. Tell me what you thought when you can.

By the same post I wrote to Mr. Barthe, asking him straight out to let me write to Marie-Antoinette. I sent him as friendly a letter as I could. What will his reply be?

I need love, Mum, on top of yours and Popo's, and it should be the love of Marie-Antoinette.

The unit I'm going to join is a good one, I might even say that at the moment it is the elite corps surpassing even the air force. There are good reasons for this. ... Mum, I also need to know for what cause I may be laying down my life. It goes without saying that I would do this for you and Popo, but there is also the love of a woman, which is worthy to be reciprocated. Am I not right, Mum, to make up my mind that she is the chosen one for me?

"The Pretty Girl from Toulouse" c.1918. (Private collection)

I look forward to hearing what you think about this, Mum. *Do you allow me to love Marie-Antoinette?* Depending on what Mr Barthe says I want us to become engaged. I am getting older, and I think about things; if I don't take this opportunity to anchor my heart I shall be capable of going astray again. Everything depends on M Barthe's reply: I'll let you know what he says.

I'm still at Gidy, and well back into the swing of things. Did you send me any money? This evening a pal will be going to Mr Boisvieux's to pick up the post, and I'm hopeful that there will be something there for me.

Goodbye, Mum, and big, big hugs,

Pierre

P.S. I've just had a great little letter from Popo. She's a hell of a girl! I'll write back to her tomorrow.

An undated postcard posted by Paulette to Pierre. Discovered among Marie-Antoinette's papers, Pierre must have kept this card, the only one of Paulette's correspondence to survive:

Dear little Pierre,

Today we were in Toulouse and thinking and talking of you. For a souvenir of our trip we sent you a little packet of "La Marquise de Sévigné".[16] You'll fancy that, I'm sure! I chose some cards and I had to send you this one of a pretty little woman. She's

16 *La Marquise de Sévigné*: A popular brand of luxury chocolates established at the turn of the last century. [T's N]

a woman from Toulouse, just like you like them! You'll like looking at her, and it will make the blues go away!

That should put a smile on your face, little soldier!

Your little sister gives you a big hug (perhaps a cuddlier one than the girl from Toulouse, eh?)

Popo

Pierre obtained leave in late June. It was during his time at Montauban that he received St Pierre's Day (29 June) salutations from his army comrades. Returning to camp, he wrote:

5 July 1918
Little Mum,

I've just got back, tired, but safe and sound at Gédy, so here's a word. The journey went well. I bumped into one of my old friends who is a law student, and we enjoyed chatting about old times. I had an excellent lunch in the restaurant car, and we spent the afternoon drinking beer and playing chess. It was brilliant.

We got to Orleans at about 5.00 in the afternoon, to find the town in the middle of celebrating the arrival of the Americans with shows and concerts. Net result I stayed there till midnight, after which I shouldered my bag and walked the 15 miles back to camp. I got back at five in the morning completely bushed, so it's a good thing today is my rest day!

That's all now. Big hugs,

Pierre

9 July 1918
I've just got your letter of the 6th, and I don't need to tell you how much I enjoyed reading it. I must reassure you that I only spent the evening at Orleans without getting involved in any amorous adventures!

Now Mum, be serious. Do you really think that me having a bit of fun means I love you less? Do you think I love those girls I knock about with?

Think it out. Remember what sort of a chap your son is, and you will at once recognise that the biggest part of my love is reserved for you and Popo. You say you live for me: don't you think I feel the same way? Haven't I often said to you that if it weren't for you and Popo, I'd have copped it a long time ago? Don't have any concern about my love for you. It means the world to me, what more can I say? Really I shouldn't love you as much as I do, because you have some serious faults, one of which is your appalling indiscretion. I'm not complaining, Mum, I just do what I have to do, and I only ask that you don't start poking your nose into my affairs again.

As you guessed, the lads were glad to see me back.

The writing paper is nice and it's a pleasure to use it.

Off now. Big hugs,

Pierre

11 July 1918

Little Mum,

In a word, I'm miserable, because I haven't had a letter from you. Nor have I had one from Marie-Antoinette. This won't do. Perhaps tomorrow? It's good to live in hope, but the fact that my little *Zinzin*[17] loves me is not quite enough.

Big kisses,

Pierre

17 July 1918

Little Mum,

At last a moment to write to you. It has been hard for me to leave you without news over the past few days. The little cards I sent to Popo don't make up for that. Your letters have arrived and done me good: believe me, however much you love your son, you are one of the ones he loves most. I say 'one of' and you will know what I mean.

I was exhausted. We shall leave the day after tomorrow with all our equipment. I now have the tank in which I shall go on to glory. Mum, the first thing I did when I got it was to fix Nénette and Rintintin on it. You can see I've made sure to do everything to smooth the way and have the best chance of success.

As to how I'm feeling, I was touched by the letter I had from Marie-Antoinette. Perhaps touched isn't quite the right word. I had to examine deep down what I felt. I feel that Marie-Antoinette loves me so well that I ought to bring myself once and for all to pledge to her a bit of my heart (the bit you'll allow me to pledge to her).

She didn't say anything to help me with my dilemma. She wants to know if I really love her before saying anything. This explains why it's taken me a week and more to think of my reply. I subjected myself to tests. I went to Orleans and even Paris looking up all my old flames (I'll tell you about the Paris trip tomorrow).

The result is that I found them all boring. I'm letting them go and I'm going to write to Marie-Antoinette tonight to tell them that I'm all hers.

She must tell me what she thinks. Because she is going to be the guiding star in my life I shall do what she wants. And to what end? To make you happy and her happy at the same time. How does that strike you? I won't go on about it anymore now, but more tomorrow. Tell me what you think.

I'm sorry I can't go and see Mr Barthe. It's quite impossible.

Let's talk a bit about Montauban. You speak of the difficulty that Bernard has had. It was to be expected, but I sympathise with you. I've had a letter from Godmother about it, too, to which I've replied. I've sent a word to Uncle Baptiste as well to cheer him up as much as possible.

That's all. Big hugs,

Pierre

P.S. My new address is A.S. 336, 12thBattalion, B.C.M. Paris.

---

17 *Zinzin*: Pierre's nickname for a tank. [T's N]

Renault FT17 Tank during training. Photos from Pierre's album. (Private collection)

9

Not yet killed or wounded

From 26 September the great Allied counter-offensive progressed across the Western Front. This resulted in 250,000 casualties evenly distributed between both sides. The 504th Assault Artillery Regiment, to which Pierre belonged, was in the forefront during this time, attached to *Groupe d'Armées des Flandres* (GAF – Flanders Army Group) in October 1918. See Appendix VI for its activities during August to October 1918.

Pierre set off for the front on 19 July. On the following day he wrote to his mother:

20 July 1918

Little Mum,

Here's a novelty. It's my first letter written from inside Zin-zin! Here we are now in the battle zone. Don't panic, Mum, there is still a while before we attack. Before that we have to practise joint manoeuvres with the infantry, so no danger.

As to our journey here, it was a shambles. You wouldn't credit what a lather we got in getting all the kit packed up. Ye Gods! This may be 'an elite corps' but it doesn't make it a cozy one. We got it all organised in the end and the actual trip went OK, and leaving Cercottes was almost nostalgic.

Here we are near our new camp, and waiting for the order to move, so I hope you'll be happy that I'm writing a few lines.

It's quite a comfortable little 'office' in here: I'm sitting on the driver's seat and leaning the writing case on the controls and writing by the dim light coming in through the little door from outside. Lots of ideas pop up easily to my mind!

I have christened my tanks: mine is called MIMI, after Marie-Antoinette (that's what everyone calls her). Its gun, which I'm going to knock the Boches over with, is called Aunt Madeleine. I've hung Nénette and Rintintin off it. The other tank, the corporal's, is called POPO. Good names, eh? With Mimi and Popo there is nothing to fear, and little Pierre will ride on to victory!

Ah, we're off, so I'll stop. I'll write to you from camp this evening.

Big kisses,

Pierre

5 August 1918

Little Mum,

I haven't had a moment to write for the last two days because we've had to move. I'll tell you another time about our stop at a station, which by a strange coincidence is in the same area where I was in 1914. Little by little we are getting nearer the action. The worst thing is that all these moves slow down the postal service terribly!

Our journey has been very pleasant. At every station we get a big welcome because everyone is curious to see the young men with their wonderful little tanks. Everyone wants to have a look at them, but sadly our "toys" are all covered over with tarpaulins.

Pierre with ashplant stick. (Private collection)

So it's the same area, with the same welcome and at the same time of year, four years on from before, so good omens for this 'new war' of mine which is about to start. I'm sure I'll be just as lucky here as I was last time.

I've got to stop now, because the train is moving again.

Big kisses,

Pierre

This letter, not in the potato sack with the others, appeared in the weekly newspaper *L'Indépendant du Tarn-et-Garonne* on 17 August. The article, signed "P.S.", was headlined *Letter from a tankman from Montauban.*

How smart our little zin-zins are as they go forward! In their green and yellow camouflage, they are soon lost among the shambles of the trench lines as they bound with surprising speed and ease across the various defensive barriers and shell craters. Each one has its battle name, nearly always the name of some woman the commander fancies, clearly marked out on its turret. The little monsters look invincible, and confident that no-one can resist them.

And then what a sight when they return! They are still a fine sight, because they are covered with the glory of having fallen in combat, but all that is left of them is a mass of carbonised iron full of shell holes. The waves of colour are gone, because the fire has burned and scorched everything. You can still see the loved one's name on it, much dimmer and sadly knocked about. It's sad indeed that it was unable to protect the two young lads who had been relying on it to keep them safe.

L'Indépendant du Tarn-et-Garonne newspaper
cutting, 17 August 1918. (Private collection)

Lettres de Soldats Montalbanais
et citations.

Lettre d'un soldat tankiste montalbanais.

... Qu'ils sont beaux lorsqu'ils partent tous nos petits zin-zins !

Camouflés jaune et vert, ils disparaissent dans le cahos des tranchées, et souples, rapides, élégants, bondissent de parapets en trous d'obus. Leur nom de bataille, presque toujours celui d'une femme aimée, se détache sur leurs tourelles. Et ces petits monstres paraissent invincibles, si sûrs d'eux-mêmes, que rien ne doit leur résister.

Et pourtant quel tableau lorsqu'ils reviennent! Ils sont beaux encore, car la gloire d'être tombés à l'ennemi les illustre. Ce n'est plus pourtant qu'un amas de ferraille carbonisée, montrant les larges plaies béantes ouvertes par les obus. Plus de couleur ondoyante, l'incendie passant par là a tout brûlé, tout roussi. Le nom chéri se distingue encore, mais si terne, si effacé, si honteux!... triste, en effet, de n'avoir pu protéger les deux petits poilus qui l'avaient pris comme sauvegarde.

L'intérieur est encore plus sinistre. Ses obus, éclatés par la chaleur, ont tout démoli; et les leviers et les commandes semblent se tordre dans une dernière convulsion...

Et deux hommes fiers et jeunes étaient là-dedans; c'était des petits tankistes, de ces nouveaux héros que le public aime et chérit... Ne méritent-ils pas toute cette admiration?   P. S.

The inside is even more fearful: the heat of the fire has set off its own magazine of shells, reducing it to a complete wreck. The levers and machinery have been contorted by this last convulsion.

Inside that tank had been two proud young men, two of those little tank men who are the new heroes the public admires so much. I think you can agree that they deserve all the admiration they get.

P.S.

Pierre Suberviolle had his baptism of fire on 1 September. August had been spent in moving around, training and giving demonstrations:

6 August 1918
We are still at camp at M ... We should have left here a fortnight ago, but that order has been countermanded, and we have to stay here for demonstrations. Every day we drive about in front of an audience of staff officers. Today we put on a show for some generals – Japanese ones!

Advancing tank column. Photo by Pierre Suberviolle. (Private collection)

Pierre still found time to write and study. On 23 August he asked his mother to "send two books – the ones covering the Bac syllabus for Plane Geometry and Spatial Geometry". He even took the time to advise on his sixteen-year-old sister's education:

24 August 1918

You ask what I think about Popo. Let her have as much freedom as possible to go off with her little friends, because she will be in good hands. You should have let her go to Biarritz. She is getting to be a big girl now, and she needs to get used to going out so that she won't look awkward.

She needs to have some life of her own to build up a store of memories and provide food for thought. She can't have that while she's tied to your apron strings, Mum. You must have noticed how dull a girl is when she's never been anywhere or done anything.

That's what I think, anyway, Mum. Let's accept that she is no longer a little kid; she knows how to dress and behave with enough discretion to be above suspicion. What do you think of this point of view?

On 27 August the advance began. The History of the 504th Assault Regiment states "on that day [?] the 335th and 336th sections gave valuable support to the 8th regiment of Zouaves and the 7th Skirmishers. The objective of the 336th was the village of Terny-Sorny just north of Soissons. This was achieved and 80 of the enemy were taken prisoner." Are these perhaps the attacks which Pierre speaks of in his letters of 3 and 6 September? History does not tell us.

3 September 1918

Little Mum,

OK so far. I haven't been killed or wounded. I've just got back from the attack and it went very well. The little good luck flag looked after me. The feeling of victory is very special, and I'll tell you more about it when I get back to base in the rear.

Saint-Géniès was wounded. His tank broke down and he got out and was shot in the side. I don't know how serious it is. On the whole, though, not too many men lost, so no need to worry. I'll tell you all about it when I've got time.

Big kisses,

Pierre

Renault FT17 tanks in action, Flanders 1918. Photos by Pierre Suberviolle. (Private collection)

Tanks column at the halt. Photo by Pierre Suberviolle. (Private collection)

6 September 1918

We've finished our R and R and are back off for another spell in the line. I'm pleased that the cold weather hasn't set in yet, particularly at night.

The main thing is, Mum, not to worry. We are leaving here, but an attack is not imminent.

Big hugs,

Pierre

That same day, a hurriedly scribbled note in pencil:

They've put back the start time by half an hour, so I can write a bit more. I'm glad to say that I've just got your registered letter of 29 August.

First serious business. I'm glad that Mr. Rigaud has gone.

As to Popo marrying a vet, that's the best solution if it's what she wants. I've still got four more years before I qualify, and it will be difficult for me to start studying again. I shall work steadily towards that provided, of course, that I get out of this. Looking at it another way, given that you have made this decision, from now on I can consider my own future plans.

About me, you can tell the Verzou girls that the good luck flag has seen me through one battle and even brought me glory. It looks as if it's going to do the trick again. Anyway, Mum, don't you fret about it.

Big kisses,

Pierre

Send the extra 100 francs I asked for, please.

In mid-September it seems that Pierre's unit was granted a few days R and R at Mailly[1], after which he was given some home leave. Returning to his unit he added a P.S. to his letter with the odd request: "Could you send me a basket of grapes?"

---

1   Mailly is located in the Champagne region just south of Rheims.

L'ÉGLISE SAINT-ÉLOI DE DUNKERQUE

Church of St Eli at Dunkirk. (*Le Miroir*, 14 January 1917)

Dunkirk, 10 October 1918

This letter is going to surprise you. It's been a few days since I wrote to you because we've been constantly on the move. The odd word here and there was not really enough, was it, Mum?

Three days after I came back off leave we did indeed depart from Mailly for ... we didn't really know where. Two days ago, on waking up on the straw covered floor of a cattle wagon, there I was near Dunkirk! I was quite pleased to find myself here again.

We got off the train about five miles from Dunkirk waiting to go up into the line (which can't be long now). I was bored in the camp, so I got a day's leave to go into Dunkirk, and I'm writing to you from one of the big cafés there. You can't imagine what an effect it had on me to see this old town again. I haven't seen it since January 1916, and after two years it was almost like coming home again.

It upset me a bit to see the damage caused by shelling in the town. It isn't the old Dunkirk happy and laughing as it used to be. I remember how all the lights came on in the evening and you used to see a crowd of pretty women, and French and English men, as well as sailors from every part of the world.

That's all over now. The windows have had their glass blown out and there is shell damage everywhere. The monuments are in a pitiable state. The Jean-Bart tower still stands impassive and seems to have escaped damage, but the cathedral is a sorry sight. Shells have completely destroyed its interior. It's pure destruction. The facade by contrast seems to have suffered little damage, and has retained its ancient majesty in defiance of the wickedness of the shells. The central door has suffered most. The two statues which flanked it have been riddled by shrapnel, and the old cathedral looks as though it is bleeding through these white pockmarks, which stand out starkly against the weathered surface of the surrounding stone, which is such a typical glory of old buildings. The old port is still the same, full of shipping decked out with the flags of different colours.

The old friend which I was most glad to see again was the sea with its beach and dunes. I felt two years younger as I walked to the end of the jetty, in the teeth of the wind off the sea. There I could see in the distance the sea; the sight re-awakened in me the memory of the adventures on all my voyages. How I still love the sea!

At my feet the waves were breaking on the rocks and spattering me with foam. Flights of seagulls swept to and fro, their guttural cries adding an extra dimension of wildness to the wild sea itself.

On the right, out of sight, was the great North Sea beach which seems to go on for ever: it's chopped up into a multitude of little waterways at low tide which disappear from view as the advancing sea overwhelms them. And further round to the right still are the dunes with their little hillocks covered with broom bushes; the wind whistles in the sand and picks up handfuls of it and deposits them fifteen feet away.

In the face of these beauties of Nature I felt myself born again. I thrilled to the feeling of déjà vu at the beauty of the sight. That's what I'm fighting for here, Mum, a country which I love, and I'll surely get through.

Big hugs from your big kid,

Pierre

The fighting increased in intensity, until news arrived that the Germans and Austrians had requested (on 4 October) American intervention on their behalf for an armistice. President Wilson had yet to reply, so the war went on.

12 October 1918

Little Mum,

Day follows day and one's feelings go on, and this happy news has been enough to lift the feeling of gloom provoked by these terrible B … n [Belgian] fogs.

The very evening I sent you the long letter from D … e [Dunkirk] we got the order to go into the line. It was enjoyable going through all the little highways and byways that I knew so well from my escapades back in 1915. The front line has moved east some distance from where it was then, so we passed through the area which has been so bitterly fought over in this horrible and appalling war. It was round here that Paul Galinier was wounded.

I have never seen such an awful place. As far as the eye can see the ground has been churned up, with shell holes everywhere. The trees have either been blown to bits or remain as nightmarish blackened stumps without any branches.

This is all very fine, but there is another aspect. All the shell holes are full of water, and so close together that it's hard to find anywhere to pitch our tent. And when we've got it up we find that the fog and damp penetrate inside to make us even more uncomfortable.

Anyway, Mum, we'll get by. Your little Pierre is always equal to what's thrown at

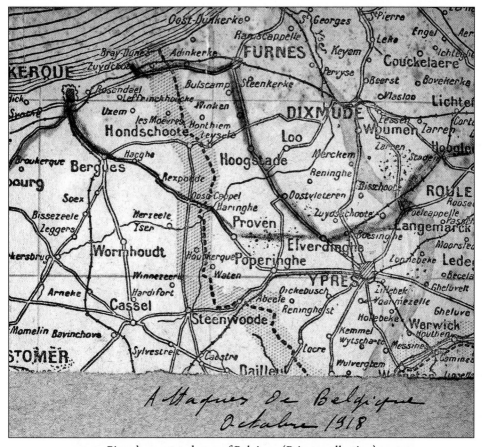

Pierre's annotated map of Belgium. (Private collection)

him, and the war's not going to last long now.
  Big kisses
  Pierre

From the History of the 504th (see Appendix V), there is confirmation of what Pierre described in his next two letters. On 14 October:

[T]he 334th and the 336th mopped up all the machine gun nests between the Roulers-Thouront Road and the Shosting-Gilberg Road. This action was swiftly undertaken and crowned with success, with the tanks playing a decisive part. When the prisoners were interrogated, it was clear that they were demoralised and quite incapable of carrying on the struggle; this in spite of the complex defensive works, including tank traps and well-camouflaged artillery pieces, which spread across the entire battlefield.

On 15 October Second Lieutenant Duprat is mentioned (as he is in Pierre's letter of 18 June); he appears to have mounted Pierre's tank only to be wounded with him.

Ruins near Roseleare (Roulers). Photos by Pierre Suberviolle. (Private collection)

British manufactured "splatter mask" issued to tank crews.
Photo by D. Labaume. (Private collection)

Captured German A7V tanks with French and American soldiers (Private collection)

14 October 1918
Little Mum,

7.00 p.m. and I've just got back from an attack. Once again I've got out of it OK, so you see there is no cause for concern. I did get hit with splinters above my right eye, which covered my face with blood, but no serious damage.

Great attack. We advanced several miles and took several villages and farms. I'll tell you all about it when I've got a moment.

Big kisses,
Pierre

The next letter, pencilled in large characters, is quite legible when considering the trying circumstances:

17 October 1918
Quartermaster

Ward 9, Hospital 34b – Postal Area 238
My Little Mum,

This time I got it! Guess where I am? Nice and warm in a fine white bed. Yes, Mum, I'm in the hospital at Zuydcoote, after being wounded quite seriously.

Briefly, I got hit by a lot of shrapnel on my forehead and in my left eye, which is I'm sure a goner. I've still got one left to write to you with, so it's turned out all right. I wrote to you on the evening of the first attack, on the 14th, when I was lightly wounded.[2] This did not stop me going into the attack on the 15th. Things were going all right when the Lieutenant's tank broke down, so he took over mine. I wanted to be in the attack so I told Dupuis (the driver) to get out and drove the tank myself. We'd hardly gone a hundred yards when ZIM-BOOM – I was hit full in the face and the lieutenant, who had also been hit, fell down inside the tank. I seem to remember reversing the tank a bit and then going to the lieutenant's aid. We went two and a half miles back before we found a first aid post. Three or four ambulances then lugged us back to Zuydcoote, a big hospital by the sea.

They will surely hack me about a bit here for a while, and then I'll be sent to a base hospital where you can come and give me a hug.

Smile, Mum! Big hugs.
Your big lad,
Pierre

General Headquarters of the Northern and Northeastern Armies
General Staff – Personnel Office

5 November 1918 – Order n° 11.252 (extract)
The Military Medal has been awarded to Quartermaster-Sergeant Pierre Suberviolle, Service Number 1054 (active) of the 336th Company of the 504th Regiment of

---

2   Pierre's wound was a common injury for light tank crews. Visibility in the Renault FT17 was very limited when the tank was buttoned up. This resulted in crewmen having to expose their heads for brief periods during combat.

Pierre's letter from the hospital at Zuydcoote. (Private collection)

Hospital at Zuydcoote. (Private collection)

Assault Artillery.

He is a warrant officer of great valour. Wounded on 14 October, 1918, in the course of an action lasting several hours, he refused to be sent back for treatment. On the following day he went into action again and led his half section bravely against enemy positions. Severely wounded a second time, he refused to leave the field until his unit's objective had been achieved.

This nomination entitles the holder to wear the Croix de Guerre with Palm.

Signed: PETAIN, Commander in Chief

Below is the certificate describing Pierre's injury and the circumstances during which it occurred:

We confirm before the witnesses whose signatures appear below that, on 14 October 1918, Quartermaster Sergeant Subviolles (sic) was wounded in the left temple by the ricochet of a machine gun bullet passing through the grill of the tank turret during the fighting at Hooglede[3] in Belgium. He was at the time in his tank and engaged in destroying an enemy machine gun nest, as he had been ordered to do.

Done at Humbeauville, 12 November 1918

Countersigned by three eye witnesses: Corporal Jean Berret, Corporal Joseph Doublier and Gunner Jean Dupuis.

The subsequent hospital certificate confirmed that Pierre's left eye had been removed.

18 October 1918

Little Mum,

I've got big news for you today. First of all I'm OK, but by God, it was hard yesterday. About five o'clock yesterday the doctor took off my dressing and they took me down to the theatre. A very nice nurse gave me chloroform, and that was that. The worst moment was when the pain woke me up in the middle of the night. We'll pass over that. In the morning the doctor found me sitting on the bed with my pipe in my mouth. He gave me an account of the operation they had carried out on me.

Don't let this upset you. First they removed my left eye, which had four wounds in it, and if they had left it there infection might have spread to the other eye.

Next they extracted the pieces of shrapnel which had hit me on the forehead and temple. For one of them they had to drill a hole with a brace and bit.

I think that's fixed it! I shall end up with some scars on my forehead and a glass eye.

That's enough of this stuff. I'm going to stay a few more days here, but no visitors allowed here. Later on I'll be sent to the rear, and then, Mum, you'll be able to come up and give me a hug. I look forward to that, as you can imagine.

Big kisses,

Pierre

---

3   Hooglede is a small village west of Roeselare (Roulers); Zuydcoote hospital, situated on the French coast, was approximately 35 miles to the west.

19 October 1918

Dear Little Mum,

The most important thing to tell you is that everything is fine. The operation went well, and I've just got to wait. Don't upset yourself. Your big lad will be quite handsome with his glass eye! The only scar I shall have is where they trepanned me to get the splinter out. If I wear a hat you won't be able to see it at all, so it will all work out OK.

I take everything cheerfully, and so must you, Mum, and I shall be happy if I know that you are proud of me. What does Grandpa think of his grandson? He may be a ruffian, but at least he has mangled his face for France. It will look pretty impressive to have my yellow medal alongside his Belfort medal on the sideboard. They are going to give me the Military Medal: I've got the papers here.

I'll tell you a bit about life in the hospital. The little tank warrant officer is already well-known: "He's a one" they say.

On the first day they brought me up to the ward on a stretcher. When it was my turn to go into the theatre, the stretcher bearers had disappeared. I'm a helpful bugger, so I just got up, walked over to the operating table and lay down on it. The doctors were astonished! On my left there was a chap with his chest open, and on the right another one with half a leg. It got to my turn, and at the end of the operating table a very nice nurse was waiting. She stroked my cheek with her hand, and said 'Poor young man': I took advantage of this by giving her pretty little hand a long kiss. I timed it well, because she was completely flummoxed and the doctors fell about laughing! Almost at once there was something like an appalling noise from town bells, and I fell asleep.

I was spark out while they took out my eye and drilled a hole in my skull. I woke up an hour later, and then I was a bit under the weather. Finally I could get some sleep and I was OK.

The following morning I was still coping OK. I woke up at seven and sat up on the bed and lit my pipe. Through the window I had a fine view over the North Sea.

When the doctor came in, he was stunned to find me like this. He almost collapsed! Then he said he wasn't used to seeing patients smoking the day after an operation like mine. We have become good friends, and he's a nice chap.

No more now, Mum, as I'm a bit tired.

Big hugs for you, Popo, Granny and Grandpa.

Pierre

21 October 1918

Little Mum,

I waited a bit longer before writing, so that they could take my dressing off. Everything has gone well and the operation has been a great success. The healing of the wound in my skull is going well and so is my eye. Not a trace of pus to be seen. The doctor was very happy and so was I.

Then I played a trick on him. I hid a mirror in my hand and when he took the dressing off I looked at myself. What a sight!

Mum, I burst out laughing. Half of my head was shaved and yellow from the iodine, so I looked like a Vietnamese! My forehead was marked with three scars with stitches. I look as though a huge millipede has walked across my head. As for my eye, it is just shut – you can't see anything there.

Pierre saved this congratulatory communiqué from General Herbert
Plumer, which is translated below. (Private collection)

Luckily I've got a bandage covering it all. Without this the other eye would not
be able to seduce the nurses! But Hey! I did well enough with my two eyes in that
direction!

Big kisses,

Pierre

P.S. I'll be here for another four or five days.

Renault FT17 Tank during training and in action. Note the captured Minenwerfer in the top right photograph. Photos from Pierre's album. (Private collection)

General Herbert PLUMER commanding the 2nd British Army to General BEGOUTTE commanding the Armed forces of Flanders:

> Dear General,
> I want to thank you for the tanks you kindly put at my disposal on 31 October 1918. They were of great value to my troops. Would you please convey to the Commanding Officer our thanks for the help given by his men. Our infantry who worked with the tanks speak with enthusiasm about the way they conducted themselves.
> General BEGOUTTE to the Officer commanding the tanks:

> I am pleased to forward you a copy of the letter sent by the General of the 2nd British Army in which he compliments the action of the Twelfth Tank Battalion. I add my own congratulations to those of the General.

> Sergeant-Major Pierre Suberviolles [sic] ... belonged to section 336 of the 12th Battalion during the Belgian Campaign.

10

For You!!!

From 28 October 1918, Pierre was transferred to a Rouen military hospital.

Telegram 28 October 1918
Condition – Excellent – send 200 francs to Quartermaster-Sergeant Suberviolle New Hospital Rouen 48 by telegram– letter follows – kisses – Pierre

29 October 1918
My Dear Little Mum,

Here I am in a different hospital, in Rouen. I've no idea why they've sent me here, but it shouldn't be for long.

First of all, Mum, my health is improving incredibly well. The doctors here are specialists from Paris and they say that everything is going well. The wound in my forehead is quite closed up and the eye is healing fast. I don't think it's worth you struggling up here, as the doctors say I shall be out in a week. I shall then be sent south to convalesce: they will organise the new eye for me down there, either at Bordeaux or Toulouse.

Getting to Rouen is difficult because the transport system is poor. I think you'll agree that it will be better if you wait till I get down there. I'm completely recovered now and just as I was before the injury, except for the head bandage. I would have appreciated a visit and a hug from you when I was at Zuydcoote, but that couldn't be.

You will have got the telegram I sent yesterday evening. I haven't got a penny on me. I was wounded on the 15th but they still haven't paid me. Luckily I had been prudent and I've managed to survive to the end of the month with the money you gave me when I was home on leave. I asked you for 200 francs: having come off the battlefield with nothing, I need to buy lots of things. I expect you will soon be sent my trunk and all my bits and pieces from the unit, and my letters. This is why, Mum, I am asking for so much.

First, write me long long letters, and then send all my post here.

Please send me my black jacket and puttees, and buy me a black beret. (You can get it at Darade's – size 57). If my trunk has arrived, please send my black trousers and yellow shoes.

Everything as quick as you can, please, Mum. I'm as dirty as a little pig. My clothes are all torn and blood-stained. In the afternoon we can get out a bit, so I'm going to try to clean myself up. If my trousers haven't arrived I shall buy some more. For the journey home I shall go on the ordinary trains via Paris, thus travelling in reasonable style.

I'm really looking forward to hugging you. Being stuck at the rear is making me fed up, and I'm beginning to be upset at the loss of the eye. Come on, Mum, send me a nice long letter to get my spirits back up, because I've got to get used to the injury.

Big hugs, Pierre

30 October 1918

Little Mum,

Quickly a note to thank you for the money which has just arrived. I've really been struggling without so many necessities. When my clothes arrive everything will be OK. At the moment I am dressed like the unfortunates you see in hospitals, but it won't be long before I give you a hug.

I was intrigued by your telegram. You didn't sign it, and finished it by saying 'See you soon'. Are you thinking of coming up? I should love it, but remember that half the fast trains aren't running, so you'd have a horrible time getting here. I'm anxious to get a letter from you.

It's quite odd, because I haven't got a clue what you have been thinking since the time I got wounded. I haven't had anything from you since you knew. How glad I shall be when I get your next letter! I shall read it over and over again and learn it off by heart! It's been a whole month since I heard from you, That's such a long time, especially now that I can think straight. After the surgery, I was rather numb, but now I feel exactly as before.

And now it strikes me that I haven't told you my news. The healing is going along very well as is the convalescence. At Zuydcoote I was comfortable with every care lavished on me, but here it isn't anything like as good. It's a military hospital in a barracks, with none of the comforts a hospital needs. The food is awful and there isn't enough of it. Luckily we can get out into the town.

How happy we shall be, Mum, to be together again round the same table, and this time not just on leave. It will be wonderful to be back again in an ordered family life, and this time for good. Just be patient for a little longer.

Big hugs,

Pierre

1 November 1918

My dear little Mum,

You say you've been ill! Mum, I'm very concerned because there are all sorts of nasty flu viruses everywhere at the moment. Fortunately Popo's letter put my mind at rest and I hope that you will be 100% again by the time I get back.

Now listen to your big boy: I'm telling you to be sensible and don't overdo things (I know you!). I want to get home and find you all sweet to welcome me back.

In particular, Mum, don't think of coming up here. The flu is having a terrible effect in Rouen (though not for us safely here in the hospital). If you come up here, eating in restaurants and staying in hotels, you will certainly put yourself at risk.

Just be patient a little longer, and soon, Mum, you will have your big lad back!

I've forgotten to tell you how I'm getting on. It's fantastic how my wounds have healed as if by magic: I am completely over the operation now. What a relief!

Big hugs (the best medicine to cure everything!),

Pierre

P.S. I went to Mass yesterday to say a prayer for dear Dad.

Pierre with bandage. (Private collection)

2 November 1918 (*message to his grandfather with enclosed portrait photo*)
I look really brave with my three medals on the left and my tank badge on the right and my head all bandaged up. Not everybody can show as much!

What is Pierre's third decoration other than the Croix de Guerre and Military Medal of which mention was made above? Later on he would also receive the inter-allied 'Victory Medal' (1926) and the Volunteer's Cross (1937). His Military Service Record Book also shows how much he had grown during his military service. He had been five feet nine when he joined up, but was five feet eleven and a half by the time the war ended. How young they were when they were sent away to war!

3 November 1918
Little Mum,
    I can't tell you how happy I was today when I got your letter, telling me that you are better, and you still love your big son.
    It was cheeky of you to ask me if I approve of what Granny has done! Mum, I am desperately looking forward to giving you a hug. I think your love towards me becomes even more precious than before. We are going to be so happy to find ourselves together again for ever, especially since, as you point out, I will surely be a bit more sensible than I was before. If not, who will have me ?
    Tell me about the Barthes. Do they know about my injury, and have they written to you? I should be glad to know what they think. It amused me to read in your letter that everyone wants to know about your big Pierre!
    I have mixed feelings. Of course I am touched, but at the same time I don't give

a monkey's. The important thing is to get home quickly to be fussed over by my little Mum and my little sister.

I have every reason to think that my return will not now be long delayed. When the doctor came round this morning he asked me where I was from and what I was doing. He seemed to take an interest in me, and he may even have received instructions about me. It could well be that I am going to be evacuated to Toulouse, since it is the centre of ophthalmic treatments for the area.

Once I am there we can organise everything.

As to my things, I've made the necessary arrangements for everything to be sent to you. They won't be able to do that until the unit has been withdrawn from the line.

I am happy that you aren't coming up here. The 'flu is still doing terrible damage. It could have been an excuse for a nice trip, but one must be sensible.

The visits which had been announced have not happened. As to health, I'm fine. They've taken a few more small splinters out of me, but nothing much.

I'm off now,

Big hugs, Pierre

4 November 1918 – Telegram from Bretigny
Shall accompany you to Rouen – send Pierre's address –I shall go alone if you can't come – Barthe

5 November 1918
My dear little Mum,

As every day, I look out for the postman, and particularly today because I know I've got a letter. And now I'm happy, as you write such lovely letters; I really needed them when I was going into battle and when I was wounded. I did not lack courage, but it was hard, I can tell you. The post from Zuydcoote has not yet reached me, but it shouldn't be long. I've made all the arrangements with the unit to send all my stuff to you.

You mention the clothes; it is clear that by the time you got the telegram it was already too late to send them. I asked you for 100 francs to buy breeches and shoes, and I should be able to get them. I've just calculated my money situation and everything is terribly expensive. I've jotted down my expenses for you to see.

I regard some of the little bits and pieces as absolutely indispensable; for example the various meals I've bought in town (because we are starved here), and such things as coffee, tobacco and walking out. It comes to around forty francs out of the total of 170.

I do hope that you will send me the money as soon as you get the telegram. It'll be really useful as I intend to spend some time in Paris on the way back and I need the money to look respectable. We aren't at the beginning of the war, and a dirty wounded man is still a dirty man. I can ask you for the money because I've heard that I'm going to have a war pension of 1,200 francs a year. Big deal!

Nothing new as to when I'll be coming home. My health is still good.

Big hugs,
Pierre

Indispensable

Rembourser camarade	20F	Tabac	10F
Envoyer Infirmier Zuydcoote	10	Café (une fois par jour)	10
Berret	10	Promenades spectacles	20
Rubans de décoration	5	Repas (5 francs par repas)	30
Insignes tank	5		70F
Gants	10		
Papier lettre	10		
Encre stylo	3		
3 Cravates	10		
Savonnette	2		
Brosse dent	6		
Pate dentif	2		
Peigne	2		
Brosses	3		
Crayon	2		
	100		

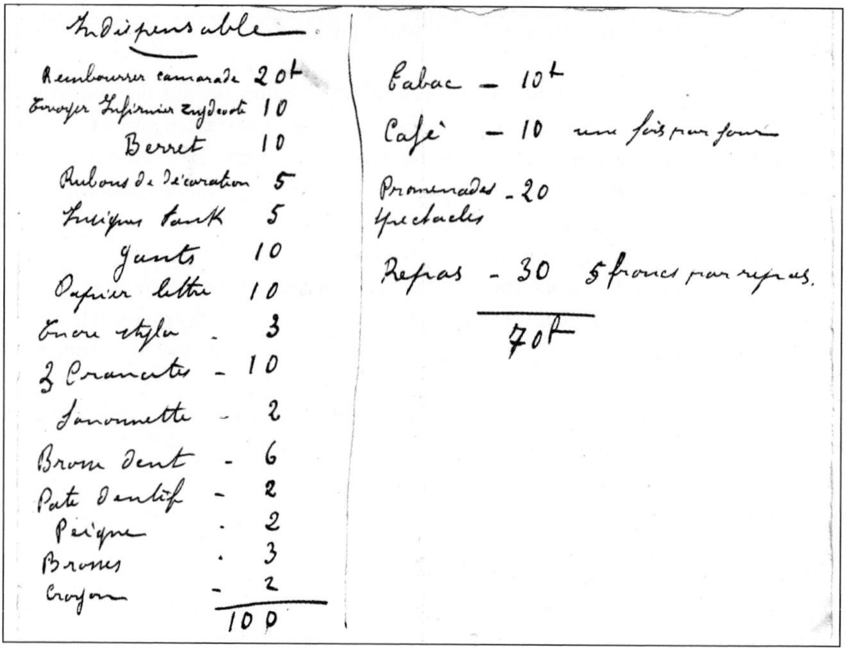

Pierre's accumulated expenses. (Private collection)

Indispensable things:

- Pay back a friend 20F
- Send to nurse at Zuydcoote 10
- Beret 10
- Medal Ribbons 5
- Tank Corps insignia 5
- Gloves 10
- Writing Paper 10
- Ink 3
- Three ties 10
- Soap 2
- Toothbrush 6
- Toothpaste 2
- Comb 2
- Brushes 3
- Pencil 2

TOTAL 100F

- Tobacco 10
- Coffee once a day 10
- Walks and sightseeing 20
- Six meals at 5F

TOTAL 70F

8 November 1918

Dear Little Mum,

HOORAY! The war is going to end and I am happy. There are English and Americans in the streets of Rouen celebrating. They are running about waving flags and they drag us along with them. The spectators look on admiringly and sometimes carry us on their shoulders in triumph.

What does it matter if I've lost an eye, Mum? I'm just happy to have given it as my contribution to the victory. The patriotism people are showing is even stronger than in 1914. Long live England! Long live America! Long live the *poilus*!

I think I've caught a bit of the madness myself!

To top it off, I'm out of here on Monday. On Tuesday I'm stopping off at Paris to see Mr Barthe and Mr Coulomb (a top specialist who is an acquaintance of his); and on Friday, THREE CHEERS, I shall be home to kiss you and hug you to death! As I've received the money I need for some fun in Paris, I'm in seventh heaven.

Great big kisses, for you on your neck, for Popo in her hair, for Grandpa on both cheeks and for Granny on the end of her nose!

Vive la France,

P. Suberviolle

9 November 1918

Dear Little Mum,

I've just been astonished to read your telegram which says 'Urgent that you go to Bretigny'. Why? You say 'Sort it out on your own', which is all very well, but I can't possibly get there before next Tuesday, the 12th.

I'm involved in a situation worthy of a novel at the moment. Thanks to Marie-Antoinette I have got to know a useful connection, Mr. Trochu, who is a captain in naval recruitment; he's a lovely chap and happy to be an intermediary between her and me. He welcomed me with open arms. This evening I am expecting a visit from Mr. Cangardel[1], Director of the Franco-American War Directorate, who will surely talk to me about Marie-Antoinette. So Mum, I hope to establish a nice home (Hum!) and perhaps end up becoming someone. All that is secret, so not a word! It belongs to the future.

They did some more fiddling about with my eye today, but it's still OK. Dear Mum, Pierre has lost an eye, but not his head!

Big kisses, and looking forward to the morning of Wednesday 13th for sure.

Pierre

The correspondence ends with five letters Pierre sent from Toulouse at the beginning of 1919:

---

1   Henri Cangardel (1881-1971) a distant married cousin of Marie-Antoinette, lived in Brétigny and she often visited him to babysit his boys aged 5 and 6 respectively. He had a brilliant merchant navy career, reaching the posts of General Transatlantic Company Administrator General at the time of the launching of the line SS *Normandie* (1932) and company president (1940). Henri never lost his great affection for Marie-Antoinette and, following Pierre's death in 1964, attempted to alleviate her grief with an all-expenses paid Mediterranean cruise. Indeed, Pierre's daughter, Jacqueline, was convinced that he was secretly in love with his cousin.

28 January 1919

Dear little Mum,

I'm in a real panic here! I went back into hospital, and they immediately popped my glass eye in! It seemed comical, you've no idea how ugly I looked! The medical people seemed to think it was OK. Anyway, Mum, you can judge for yourself as soon as I can escape!

I've done everything I can to organise the paperwork for my discharge. I think I shall have it only for about ten days. It is certain that I shan't have to do any service in the military reserve, so I don't think there's any point in going to see Mr Casaubon. I shall do some research and let you know the names as soon as I can.

The fact that I was late did not create any difficulty. As soon as I reached the hospital three young nurses who I did not know at all burst out 'Hey! Here comes young Mr Pierre!'

So I've hardly been here a moment and I am already well-known! I'm going to annoy everyone, especially Miss Quillet.

The main thing about the discharge is that it doesn't drag out too long. As for a visit, I'm afraid it's still out of the question. I can see that I am going to have to resort to some dirty tricks to be able to get out a bit.

It's quite funny, Mum: I'm writing to you from (*a café called*) 'The Americans' and it seems to me that everyone is looking at my face; they are staring at my eye, and it's getting rather boring. It doesn't bother me overmuch, with my 'can't give a toss' attitude, and I get my own back by making fun of others. Don't you think, Mum, that they are not as comical as me? Thus I have succeeded in being original!

I'll leave it at that. Big hugs.

Pierre

29 January 1919

Little Mum,

I was hoping to come and see you this evening, but have been frustrated, as I have to stay in hospital. They have to take a photograph of me to put in my discharge file. This delicate operation ought to have taken place this evening, but it has been postponed, perhaps until tomorrow morning, perhaps tomorrow evening. I have to be here for it, so I can't get away.

I'm looking forward to coming: I'm getting very depressed in here. I can't get used to life in hospital, living in this horrible dormitory and eating the abominable food. When on earth will I be finished with it all?

My eye seems to be OK. They all say they don't notice it, but I think I look awful. Mum, I'll stop there. My head is empty this evening. I'll write more in a bit.

Big hugs,

Pierre

Preserved by Marie-Antoinette – therefore one of several rare letters kept by Pierre – is a fragment of correspondence from his mother:

How can you think that you are not good-looking with your glass eye? You know that you are always handsome! You think you are disfigured, but that feeling will pass when you can try a selection of them; we'll soon find you an eye as shining and bright and saucy as the other! Even if it falls a bit short of that, the look in your good eye will be enough to win over everyone you meet.

I'm sure you're looking forward to showing your eye to Marie-Antoinette to know what she thinks of it, if that matters more to you than your mother's opinion.

3 February 1919
My Dear Little Mum,

I've just come out of the bedroom which is bitterly cold, and here, with a hot cup of lime tea, I'm writing a line to you.

I've just written a long letter to Marie-Antoinette in which I have poured my heart. There does remain just a little corner of it reserved for you, so that you won't be jealous.

Nothing new to tell you. Nothing happening at the hospital. My papers still haven't come through. I've bought a new glass eye which is miles better than the other one; it's a little bit smaller, but quite presentable.

On Thursday I'd like to go to Mas, always assuming that I can. What do you say?

Finish now.

Big hugs,

Pierre

Sunday 9 February 1919
Little Mum,

Today it is Sunday and you can imagine that I am bored. I wanted to come but I got the jitters. My return has gone smoothly thanks to a little doctor I know. He told the medical director that he had taken me into the operating theatre two mornings running 'to help him'! That worked very well (and so the operation was done). We seem to have got away with it, and now I just need to stay quiet for a few days[2].

They took my photograph again yesterday evening, and once again they made a mess of it. I was so annoyed that I found a photographer myself to do it; that will advance my discharge file by a week.

I'm also giving more thought to how I use my time and from tomorrow I'll be getting down to some serious study. I'm going to do it so much more willingly because I know that if I succeed ... . Yes, I'll study hard to reach my marriage.

You know, little Mum, that I recognise that I love Marie-Antoinette. I can't go five minutes without thinking of her. Wherever I am, I get bored and I fall to thinking 'If Marie-Antoinette were here, it would be different'.

I'm really happy to find, Mum, that although each day I see those girls who used to be my downfall, and they make eyes at me, I've had it with them. (It's goodbye, Mr Flirt: I just look back at them calmly and coldly.) So now I'm happy in myself.

I hope you will do me the honour of sending me some of your fine prose, and in expectation of that I pounce on you for a kiss.

Your big lad,

Pierre

---

2 It appears Pierre was still awaiting demobilisation, which explains his restricted movements and controlled convalescence.

Pierre and Marie-Antoinette, spring 1919. (Private collection)

18 February 1919

Little Mum,

Here I am back in Toulouse after a great time spent at the Mas, as you will have gathered from our telephone conversation.

Leaving Montauban Station was eventful, as I had to get into the carriage through the window. At Dieupentale[3] we travelled on the top of a mail-coach. Marie-Antoinette was scared stiff, but I held her in my arms. As the old coach trundled out to Mas, we had plenty of canoodling time. We had such a wonderful time there that I was not at all happy at having to leave.

Here nothing to report. They still haven't sent me to the discharge centre as there is still no room there, and it is still irritating.

While I'm delayed like this, it would be really nice if you came to see me. Be quick and drop me a line to say that you will venture out of Montauban and make your lad happy. In return I shall be happy to go shopping with you!

Big hugs,

Pierre

I've attached my photo.

---

3   With a railway station conveniently close to Mas-Grenier, Dieupentale was approximately 10 miles south of Montauban.

 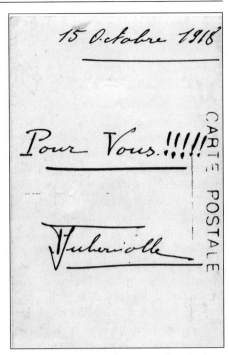

Pierre's medical file portrait endorsed "For You !!!!!" on the reverse. (Private collection)

Epilogue

Pierre Subervolle married Marie-Antoinette Barthe at Mas-Grenier on 21 May 1919. Without employment, but benefitting from his 'grand-blessé' status,[1] the couple honeymooned in Marseilles, a city the happy groom wanted to show his young bride. Setting up house in Toulouse, Pierre continued with his veterinary studies, graduating at the top of his class in October 1919. Remaining in Toulouse for two years, their daughter Jacqueline, my mother, was born on 7 February 1920.

The Toulouse years were very happy according to Marie-Antoinette. The couple returned to Rue Pouvillon in Montauban in order to take the reins of the family veterinary practice from grandfather Viguier (d. 1924). Two trying years followed. Pierre, obliged to juggle his time between studying and on-the-job training, finally qualified as a veterinarian in 1924.

Living with Augusta, however, proved increasingly difficult. Dominant within her own household, she constantly interfered in Pierre's affairs. My mother recalled (2011) their heated verbal disputes, and for the remainder of her life my mother had a phobia about screaming. Paulette, marrying at young age, also settled in Montauban. In the end, due to ongoing tensions with her son, Augusta went to live with her daughter.

Life went on. It was not easy for Pierre, who never gained much satisfaction from his work which, given the demands of the rural clientele, was exhausting and unrewarding. They were not well-off, but he occasionally allowed himself a small luxury. Indeed, in the dusty recesses of an old cupboard at Mas-Grenier, I recently discovered two small bottles of "Jicky" by Guerlain.[2] On enquiry, my mother explained that Pierre would often rub his hands with this popular cologne following a difficult animal birth.

My grandparents could not afford many holidays beyond an occasional trip to Toulouse. Pierre took great pleasure in recounting one of these visits during which he took Marie-Antoinette to the opera in the Capitole Opera House.[3] Dressed to the nines, they roared off in their open-top sports car for a big night out. On the Capitole steps they encountered one of Pierre's notable clients, the Marquis of S ... who stopped them and said: "Ah, Doctor Subervolle, I'm very glad to see you, because one of my cows ..." Pierre interrupted at once, drawing himself up to his full height and, regarding the marquis with disdain, said: "Dear Marquis, I hope your cow snuffs it!" Sweeping his white silk scarf back over his shoulder (a gesture he demonstrated whenever telling the story) he purposefully strode up the staircase!

The Second World War followed, and his daughter Jacqueline, now married to a career army officer, was on her own and residing with her parents for the duration. It was a dangerous time, and Pierre kept a revolver inside the desk in his study. One day in January 1943, whether by clumsiness or lack of attention to firearm safety, the weapon discharged and took off a finger of his left hand.

---

1 Grand-blessé: Literally a "Great Wounded One". The term suggests admiration for an individual who has been wounded fighting for his country. There is no English equivalent.
2 Expensive cologne introduced in 1889. Still in production, it was once popular with Sean Connery.
3 Situated at Toulouse Central Square, this magnificent 18th-century edifice was designed to house opera and town hall under one roof.

Pierre and Marie-Antoinette May 1919. (Private collection)

Pierre following his revolver accident. Drawing by Jacqueline
Suberviolle-Labaume c. 1943. (Private collection)

Pierre c.1960. (Private collection)

Despite this second injury, Pierre continued to work, visiting his daughter and son-in-law in Austria and Morocco on occasional holidays. Retiring to Mas-Grenier, Pierre died there in 1964. Marie-Antoinette joined him in the village cemetery in 1991.

Appendices

I

French Rations

There were three types of rationing (normal, strong, reserve) in the French Army during the First World War. Normal was allocated during periods when troops were not subjected to severe stress. Strong was allocated during lengthy marches or combat; emergency rations when steady supplies were unavailable.

The 'strong' ration for one day consisted of 750 gm of ordinary bread or 700 gm of biscuit bread; 500 gm of fresh meat; 100 gm of dried vegetables or rice; 20 gm of salt; 32 gm of sugar; 24 gm of roasted coffee either as grains or in tablets; and 30 gm of lard. Normal rations consisted of the same variety of foodstuffs, but in slightly smaller quantities. Reserve rations consisted of 300 gm of "war-bread" in six rolls; 300 gm of tinned seasoned meat; 80 gm of sugar; 36 gm of coffee; 50 gm of salted soup; and 625 ml of *eau-de-vie*[1] to act as a stimulant.

Rations were distributed each night; fresh meat after dusk; bread, lard and sundry items the following morning. Poilus carried all of this in addition to two days reserve rations, which were to remain uneaten until sanction from their commanding officer. This would only be given if active service exigencies prevented regular distribution of normal rations.

The vehicle convoys were a vital link in the supply chain between the food warehouses, the stations, the cook-houses and the front itself, which moved according to the fortunes of war. Vehicles were limited to trips of just under 50 miles.

(*Lectures pour Tous* – 1 January 1915)

---

1   *Eau-de-Vie*: "Water-of-life": a distilled beverage made from fruit other than grapes.

II

SS *Theodore Mante*

The 3,500 ton steamer SS *Theodore Mante,* Pierre's mode of transport to Salonika, was built in 1912 and operated by a Marseilles shipping company. At 320 feet long and 50 feet wide, this fine ship had made 28 previous voyages during its eight months' war service. It was named after its shipping magnate owner, Theodore Mante; in 1916 he was court-martialed and found guilty of collaborating with the enemy. The ship was subsequently requisitioned by the Naval Ministry, which renamed it SS *Mustapha II* in 1917. Refitted as an auxiliary cruiser with four guns and minelaying capabilities, the *Theodore Mante*, rechristened the *Djebel Antar* in 1933, spent the next four years as a merchant vessel before its sale to Billmeir & Co (London) where the ship was operated under the name of SS *Helendra*.

Journal d'Elie Burnod
from the internet

III

Salonika 1914

Salonika is a city of great strategic and commercial significance for central Europe, and many bitter conflicts have raged for its possession. It is one of the main ports through which trade passes into Central Europe from the Orient via the isthmus of Suez, and since 1880 via the Suez Canal.[1] Situated at the head of an inlet which reaches far inland, it is a well-protected deep-water port big enough to accommodate whole fleets of ships. For these reasons it was one of the most famous cities of the ancient world. Despite the anti-commercial stance of the Ottoman regime, it remained a large and populous city with a real port. From Salonika a railway line ran up to Belgrade and from there to central Europe; another line linked it to Constantinople. A third line went to Monastir, and would eventually link it to Athens. No city of the Eastern Mediterranean could look forward to a brighter future than Salonika.

On the other hand, its resources were limited. Throughout the war the powers who fought there had to bring everything they needed with them, including men, horses, food supplies, medical supplies and munitions. Everything had to come by sea, and the great bay suddenly became a hive of activity as never before.

Salonika began life as Therma, a port of the great Macedonian King Philip, the father of Alexander the Great. It was later incorporated into the Roman and Byzantine empires, utilised by the crusaders and captured by the Venetians before falling to the Ottoman Turks in the 15th century. It provided a sanctuary for Jews expelled from Spain by the Christians after 1492, and they constitute half of its 150,000 inhabitants today.

The city had only recently become part of Greece as a result of the Second Balkan War (1913) fought between Bulgaria and Greece over territories formerly ruled by the Ottomans. Without the presence of the Allies, it would become Bulgarian again, or rather German, since Germany very much wanted to control this pearl of the Eastern Mediterranean.

Salonika was a pearl in the commercial sense, but in common with most of the other cities of the Eastern Mediterranean its picturesque appearance concealed shambolic streets and an unhealthy reality. From a distance with its minarets, roofs and ancient walls by the seashore, Salonika made a deep impression on visitors. ... It is an astonishingly cosmopolitan melting pot where Jews, Greeks, Rumanians and Slavs mingled with the almost equally diverse troops in the French and British armies. Among the French forces, apart from men from France itself, there were Arabs and Kabyles from Algeria and Tunisia, Moroccans, negroes from the Sudan and creoles from the Caribbean. Among the British forces there were Scottish Highlanders in their kilts, Australians, New Zealanders and Indian army soldiers of several different races. The Serbs and Montenegrins who trickled in to join the allies increased the proportion of Slavs.

The ethnic mix of the town is no less complex than its architecture. It has an ancient triumphal arch known as Alexander's Arch, a medieval keep known as the White Tower topped with crenellated battlements, mosques, Greek Orthodox churches dating from the Byzantine era and synagogues. Its 'souks' (markets) are a joy to behold if not for the smell. It

---

1   Salonika, like Venice and for exactly the same reasons, was important for two thousand years or more before the Suez Canal was built.

is all unmistakably Middle-Eastern except for the cinemas which have sprung up everywhere.

The harbour is the reason for the town and its primary source of income. It was constructed by French engineers who provided it with 1250 yards of quays. Standing up thirty or forty feet from the sea-bed, these quays allowed large vessels to dock, where previously there had only been a marina for small craft. The allied forces improved the port further by the construction of cranes and railways. The improved port was able to deal quickly with the troops, guns, cars, horses, cattle and other paraphernalia required by the armies. The most vulnerable western section of our trenched encampment, where the road and railway lead away to Monastir, is well protected by the guns of the naval ships moored in the anchorage.

Taken from an account of the war, up to December 1914, by Ardouin-Dumazet, titled 'The War: documents of the photographic section of the French Ministry of War' (1915). The section above is from the Introduction to volume 3.

IV

The Macedonian Front 1916-17

Fighting round Florina and Monastir, September 1916 to April 1917

The Bulgarians held the mountains standing over Florina* in the northwest of Greece. These included the western massif towards Lake Prespa* (Presba) and the Kaïmatchalan. The Bulgarians had invaded Greek territory on 17-18 August, and at the same time moved into Eastern Macedonia, both moves forming part of a joint attack on the Salonika camp. On 28 August, the Rumanians entered the war on the Allied side. At first the Allied forces remained on the defensive, but on 10 September General Sarrail ordered an attack towards Florina, and this succeeded in taking the town on 17 September.

The Cerna Loop

In October 1916 the Allies continued to attack the Bulgarian lines. Despite receipt of reinforcements, they did not succeed in breaking through the Bulgarian lines. They suffered heavy losses and accordingly gave up the offensive, settling into defensive positions. Towards the east of the sector the British General Milne's forces secured the area about Struma.

December 1916

The British took the offensive, and the Albanians under Essad Pasha fought the Bulgarian nationalist 'comitadjis'. General Sarrail was therefore engaged on a front that stretched from Chalcedon in the east to Albania in the west.

Winter 1916-17

The morale of the Allied force was low as a result of the weather, heavy loss of life during the late offensives and disease.

Albanian campaign December 1916 to May 1917

After the successful Brusilov offensive by the Russian forces north of the Carpathians (June 1916), Rumania entered the war on the side of the Allies on 28 August 1916. They launched an attack into Transylvania, assisted by the Russians. After initial success they were caught in a pincer movement between the German General Falkenhayn to the north and the Turko-Bulgarian force led by the German Mackensen to the south. Bucharest fell and the Central Powers acquired an important resource for wheat production, along with oil fields, thereby balancing the effect of the Allied naval blockade of German seaports.

The Rumanian defeat dashed any chance of success for the Allied Forces in Macedonia. General Sarrail's men put up a sturdy resistance to Bulgarian attacks, and the French and the Serbs together seized Monastir on 19 November 1916, which was their first strategic success. The army then fell back on to the defensive and consolidated.

The occupation of Valona (20 December 1916)

Italian forces landed in the Bay of Valona as a preliminary to their conquest of southern Albania.

Note: * denotes places and people mentioned in Pierre's correspondence

Santi Quaranta
The Italians advanced at Santa Quaranta and then turned north to Koritza.

Koritza
The 76th Infantry Division, which had just disembarked in Salonika, advanced towards Albania in the area of Koritza and then d'Erseck prior to making contact with Italian forces. This opened communications between Valona and Koritza, which in turn enabled Monastir to be supplied through Florina.

Hill 1248
In March the 57th, 76th and 156th Infantry Divisions assaulted the high ground at Peristeri and Hill 1248 to link up with forces round Lake Presba and Okrida. The attack failed. Thus the Allies were unable to relieve Monastir.

Spring 1917
Attacks had little success and were attended with heavy losses; Allied forces lost ground.

The Greek campaign and entry into Athens
Conquest of Thessaly. Given the pro-German attitude of King Constantine, General Sarrail recommended the use of force. He dispatched troops by rail to seize Thessaly, taking Larissa, Corinth and Athens. Larissa fell on 11/12 June, then Trikala to the west. The forces involved went on to seize control of the Corinth Canal.

Events in Athens (March 1916-December 1917)
French marines disembarked forces at Piraeus between 10 and 12 June. Major political upheaval was taking place in the city. The French seized control of the Bay of Salamis and occupied Zappeion Hill and Piraeus. Jonnart, the French High Commissioner, met Zaimis, the newly appointed Greek Prime Minister, and presented him with an ultimatum that King Constantine must abdicate.

Camps around Salonika
These were established in marshy areas and occupied a wide swathe of territory around Salonika. The camps at Ambelones and Sedkes were for the Serbian troops, the one at Hortiak for the French and the one at Lembet for the English. The camp at Zeitenlik accommodated Serbs, British, French and Vietnamese, and outside it there was a gypsy camp. At Topcin displaced Greeks put up tents near the Vietnamese and Serbs.

Salonika hospitals
The Salonika base was defended by trenches dug by the soldiers as their daily activity; at night they returned to the disease-ridden camps. The sick were dealt with in field hospitals organised in makeshift tents. The dead were buried in the cemetery at Zeitenlik. Soldiers wounded at the front were accommodated in hospital ships moored in the harbour. The staff aboard these ships only performed surgical operations. Those soldiers who died of their wounds were buried at sea.

Médiathèque de l'architecture et du patrimoine
<http: mediatheque-patrimoine-culture.gouv> (May 2010)

Salonika became more than ever a secondary theatre in which the troops had to fight an equal struggle against their official enemy and a second one – disease. Illness affected 360,000 men, almost 95 percent of the total engaged. Dysentery, scurvy and venereal diseases were common, and treated only with a limited and poorly equipped medical service. The worst problem was malaria, which was endemic in the region, its last foothold in Europe, and had spread dramatically in the early years of the 20th century. The Balkan wars, which had involved people of all the peninsula's different races, made the area ideal for the spread of epidemics.

It was clearly a problem for the army waging war with a large proportion of its men hospitalised and the rest in a state of generally poor health. Emergency measures were taken to care for the sick and remove the environmental conditions (the marshy areas) which encouraged disease. As a result malaria was wiped out in Macedonia.

Chemins de mémoire <http://www.cheminsdememoire.gouv.fr/> (May 2010)

Note: * denotes places and people mentioned in Pierre's correspondence

V

Tank Force Training Centre in 1918

Tank unit personnel, recruited from many different branches of the French Army, were trained at Cercottes Camp.* The establishment of a course of instruction was made difficult due to the lack of available tanks, and was therefore rudimentary. Organisers also encountered accommodation difficulties for the men put in their charge.

It is pleasant to record that with goodwill on all sides, the difficulties were overcome. Infantrymen, cavalrymen, gunners, sappers and drivers were organised by officers who had to master the necessary skills themselves before passing them on to their men. Their hard work resulted in the rapid formation of a force with a common skill base, so that in just a few weeks the regiment reached a state of combat readiness in which its leaders could lead and uphold the honourable traditions of the branches of service they were recruited from. The period of the war during which the 504th regiment was raised was one in which bitter fighting drained the existing resources of the nascent tanks force. Therefore, it was essential that armoured units were prepared to take the field as soon as possible.

Historiques de régiments <http.jeanluc.dron.free.fr/th:historiques>
(Accessed April 2010)

Note: * denotes places and people mentioned in Pierre's correspondence.

VI

History of 12th Battalion, 504th Regiment of A.S. (*Artillerie Spéciale*)

On 16 June 1918, the 12th Battalion was formally constituted (at Gidy* near Orleans, rather than at Cercottes); Commander Chaigneau assumed command. He began his training with firing drill on the ranges at Cercottes, and this was continued at Bourron, where the unit was moved in July. After a brief stay there they moved, on 3 August, to Poivres, the camp at Mailly*, for joint manoeuvres with the infantry. While there, they provided demonstrations to visiting American and Japanese military missions and completed preparations for active service. The order was communicated to hold themselves ready to move on 26 August, and on that day Captain Gaillard's 334th Company, Lieutenant Deau's 335th and Lieutenant Barrière's 336th* did indeed entrain at Poivres for movement to La Vache Noire just east of Vic-sur-Aisne. The 335th and 336th came under the command of Major Roussy, who was the officer commanding French tanks in the American Expeditionary Force sector.

That same day, the 335th and 336th provided effective support for the 8th Zouave Regiment and 7th Regiment of Skirmishers. The 335th took Neuville-Margival and the tunnel of Vauxaillon. It destroyed numerous machine-gun nests at the cost of seven of its tanks. The 336th succeeded in taking Terny-Sorny (north of Soissons) with 80 prisoners.

After a series of marches and countermarches around Montecorne, Juvigny and Pommiers, the battalion reformed at Vézaponin and entrained at Vic for the journey to Humbauville where it prepared for its next action. After a short rest the 12th was called upon to undertake another difficult assignment. It unloaded its tanks at Bergues (Nord) and camped near Ypres in Belgium.

An offensive against Theilt et de Grand was planned for 14 October.* This would be undertaken by a combined force of British, French and Belgian troops, assisted by the 77th D.I. The 77th was tasked with taking the plain of Hooglede* and the heights of Coolscamp. At H-hour the tank sections set off in the direction of Gilsberg and Gils. The St. Chamond tanks were incapable of traversing the marshy area north of the Staden-Roulers road, and the infantry were held in front of Hooglede. The 335th intervened thus enabling the infantry to pass east of the village.

At 13.30 two sections of the 335th, which had taken positions behind the ridge at Hooglede, moved to the attack with the 97th R.I. Passing over the ridge to the north, they proceeded on a line parallel to the Roulers-Thourout road. Their aim was to come back into action in the direction of Schosting, cutting the enemy's line of retreat. This was successful, and by 15.00 hrs all enemy resistance had ceased. A third attack was then undertaken. The order came at 16.30 to move to the Gitsberg-Schosting front with the remaining five tanks. These were to rendezvous at nightfall west of Hooglede after eliminating all the machine-gun nests between the Roulers-Thourout and Schosting-Gitsberg roads.

In this rapid and successful action, the role of the tanks was decisive. Interrogation of prisoners revealed their demoralisation and feeling that further struggle was useless despite the complex defensive works. These consisted of cleverly camouflaged tank traps and artillery which extended in-depth across the defensive zone.

It seems likely that Pierre was involved throughout the day's fighting. His wound certificate states that he had been hit (not seriously according to his own account) on the 14th at 07.20 hrs. His letter that evening also states: "It's seven o'clock. Attack over. I managed to get myself out all right again."

During the night of 14/15 October, the 334th and 336th assembled west of Hooglede. At 04.15, the 336th was ordered to cooperate with two battalions of 97th R.I. in taking Gilsberg and its railway station. Zero hour was fixed for 07.00. Although prior reconnaissance of the ground proved impossible, both sections reached the start line. Lieutenant Duprat's* section's objectives were the woods and farms south and south-west of Gist and Tinance. The section commanded by Lieutenant Levillain was to seize the northern part of Gitsberg, the main road to the east of it, the railway line and the southern part of the railway station. Intense fighting followed; four tanks were knocked out during the first hour. Lieutenant Levillain's tank struck a landmine on the level crossing; two other vehicles had their fuel tanks punctured by enemy fire, and a fourth was crippled by a pierced radiator. Despite these losses, the enemy was forced to retire.

The 336th (without Pierre) continued in action until 17 October.

Historiques de régiments <http.jeanluc.dron.free.fr/th:historiques>
(Accessed April 2010)

Note: * denotes places and people mentioned in Pierre's correspondence